10,000 MILES WITH 10,000 REASONS

A JOURNEY INTO THE HEART OF AFRICA

Nancy Frantz

The proceeds from the book will be donated toward a project to provide an ongoing supply of food for the orphans in the village.

eLectio Publishing

Little Elm, TX

www.eLectioPublishing.com

10,000 Miles With 10,000 Reasons
By Nancy Frantz

Copyright 2017 by Nancy Frantz. All rights reserved.
Cover Design by eLectio Publishing.

ISBN-13: 978-1-63213-342-7
Published by eLectio Publishing, LLC
Little Elm, Texas
http://www.eLectioPublishing.com

Printed in the United States of America

5 4 3 2 1 eLP 21 20 19 18 17

The eLectio Publishing creative team is comprised of: Kaitlyn Campbell, Emily Certain, Lori Draft, Court Dudek, Jim Eccles, Sheldon James, and Christine LePorte.

Publisher's Note
The publisher does not have any control over and does not assume any responsibility for author or third-party websites or their content.

Contents

Acknowledgments

To Kerry, my faithful husband and constant companion, who never wavered as he followed the calling across the world.

To Cassie, Nathan, Bethany, and Brittany, who encouraged, supported, and prayed for the children's adoptions and unselfishly embraced new siblings.

To Betsy, my honest friend, who spent endless hours marking with a red pen!

Preface
by Bryan Chapell

No scriptural truth is more precious than the promise that God has adopted all who are united to Jesus Christ by faith into his family. We are no longer strangers and foreigners in Christ's kingdom but by his intercession have spiritual access to the throne room of his Father and are counted as members of his household (Eph. 2:18-22).

As Christ's love embraces us in our brokenness, as his sacrifice washes us of our sin, and as his righteousness covers the rags we have claimed for spiritual clothing, he is not ashamed to call us his brothers and sisters. And the Heavenly Father, by whose power the universe was brought into being and continues to reflect his power, allows us simply to call him Abba, Father (Rom. 8:15).

I did not feel the significance of the privilege of calling the Creator and Judge of the world "Abba" until one of my first trips to Jerusalem. There, crushed by crowds in the narrow streets of the ancient city's bazaars, my legs were brushed by the flight of a low running child who had lost sight of his parent. Heedless of the people towering above him, the child ran headlong through the thicket of legs in the direction he had last sighted his father. And as he ran, he cried for his father's attention, saying, "Abba, Abba."

Only then did I understand. "Abba" just means "daddy." The words that I had read so many times in Scripture, and logically explained to others to be a Middle-eastern term of familiarly and endearment, now really spoke to my heart as the Bible intended. The Heavenly Father has so loved us who were sin-sick and world-weary that we can crawl into the lap of his love with the familiarity and confidence of a child who has no doubt of his daddy's love.

Over and over the Bible returns to the theme of believers' adoption to signal the meaning of God's grace to the depth of our hearts. And, knowing the power of that theme to communicate the Gospel, the writers of Scripture repeatedly remind us that no human action better reflects the Gospel that inviting children in need into our families.

Still, it is one thing to give assent to this truth and quite another thing to act upon it by actually adopting a child. As Nancy Frantz writes what it has meant for her family to act upon their Gospel convictions not only by adopting one child but also by raising a "second family" for the sake of eternal souls, the Gospel shines with rare clarity. Her words will inspire you. The scriptural passages that motivated her and her husband Kerry will become more dear to you.

This story of how they crossed continents and cultures to claim the children the Lord put upon their hearts brought me more tears and laughter than I ever anticipated. And the children they now call sons and daughters for Christ's sake thrill my heart as their experience of the Gospel inspires and instructs many families in our church. Through them we know so much more of the wonder of the Heavenly Father's adoption of all who unite their eternal destinies to faith in his Son.

Chapter 1
A Single Need, a Single Soul

As I walked along the dirt path, dust rose from the unpaved road as children came out of their huts and scurried around me like mice. A tall, white woman was an unusual sight in the Baluba village in Zambia, Africa, especially a woman rich enough to have her own pair of shoes! The children were happily chattering in the Bemba language, thrilled to catch the rare glimpse of a foreigner entering their isolated and desolate village.

The unfamiliar sights and odors were more than my senses could take in at one time. The odors of smoldering logs permeated my clothes as smoke lingered over the huts. The scent of putrid wood and balmy brush made my head swirl. Tiny, grass-roofed huts dotted the countryside, providing little shelter from the winter rains. Walking down a narrow, winding path, my eyes scanned the huts for a trace of running water or electricity. Astonishingly, not a hint of light shone from the open windows. I had traveled back in time to a more primitive era, reminiscent of life many centuries ago.

As I strolled deeper into the village, a subtle quietness filled the air. Unclothed children played with sticks along the roadside while women squatted in the dirt to cook over open fire. Despite the faint noise from daily activity, I was puzzled by the stillness in the village. Dodging potholes and embedded rocks, I strolled quietly trying to make sense of it all. The sounds of motors and vehicles are nonexistent, but surely there should be evidence of wildlife, I thought to myself. There was not a single bird perched in the luscious brush, nor did I spot so much as a sparrow fluttering from the avocado tree to the mango tree. I sadly deduced that the villagers had hunted and consumed all of the local birds and animals for a source of protein. I could not fathom the magnitude of desperation in this village. Suffering is what I sensed, like a hungry lion ready to pounce on its prey. Sadness and sickness seemed to hover over the huts as the angel of death did in Egypt during the time of Moses.

Then one of the toddlers stopped playing and looked up at me. As our eyes locked, his expression was one of deep suffering and sorrow. A bulging belly, eyes glazed over, and ankles the size of my thumb told the story of anguish in his little life. Every motherly instinct in me wanted to scoop him up and give him all the love and food he needed, but I realized he was just one child out of one-and-a-half million orphans in Zambia. In the midst of this despair, other children from the village ran up to me, squealing with delight! Amidst their agony was an inner joy; their expressions and attitudes were like twinkling stars glowing in the darkness. Despite my longings, I realized I needed to lay aside my emotions and focus on my mission to rescue three orphans in the village: Andre and Andrew Mumba and Victoria Chisanga.

When this adventure began four years prior, Kerry, my husband of twenty-five years, and I were living the American dream. Although content as a typical middle-class family of five in rural America, we were rapidly approaching empty nest status. My parenting role was diminishing as our three children sprouted their wings. Surprisingly, I yearned to parent more children. I was bewildered by the nurturing feelings that resurfaced with a vengeance. My attempts at extinguishing the desire to parent once again only caused the flame to burn even brighter. Churning inside my heart was a dream to take care of more children.

One day, I was conversing with a friend and shared my longing to expand my family. I passionately stated, "I feel that I am on the edge of a cliff, and there is a veil shielding what is on the other side of the valley. There is someone waiting on the other side, but I do not know who it is."

The next morning began like a typical school day. As a teacher of the visually impaired, I began the day instructing one of my students. During the lesson, I was startled by a page from Susan, the school social worker. Returning her call, I detected urgency in her voice. She said, "Nancy, there is a fourth grade student named

2

Brittany in need of a good home, a permanent home. Would you take her in?" Standing in the hallway, speechless, I immediately realized that the Lord was leading Kerry and me to take in this child and provide her with a permanent home.

While I wanted to immediately answer with a resounding "Yes!", I told her I needed to discuss this with my husband. Hanging up the phone, I immediately called Kerry. While dialing, I contemplated what to say to break the news to him.

"Kerry, can you talk?" I inquired.

"I am in a meeting; I can't talk," Kerry said flatly.

"Before I let you go, there is a fourth-grader in need of a home. Do you want to take her in to live with us?"

Without hesitation, Kerry said matter-of-factly, "Sure. I have to get back to the meeting."

As I walked back to the classroom, I chuckled to myself. "Kerry spends more time picking out a pair of tennis shoes than adding another child to our home!"

That afternoon, Susan took me to the local theater in Princeton, Illinois. Brittany was on her very first field trip to the movie theater. As I walked into the lobby, a sea of children was excitedly milling around. Never having met Brittany, I searched for the face of a girl I thought might be her. As I entered the theater, I caught a glimpse of a girl with short hair, wearing a pink coat. "That's her!" Susan said excitedly, pointing to Brittany. She rushed me over to the young child. Brittany was so excited at the thought of seeing her first movie that her eyes looked to and fro, unable to lock eyes with mine as we were introduced. Then she turned and walked away into the swarm of students who were all buzzing around like bees. I thought to myself, "I hardly caught a glimpse of Brittany. How will she ever understand that she may end up living with us?"

The next day, Kerry decided to travel an hour away to visit Brittany. We took her swimming at a local indoor pool, and she quickly began to warm up to us. As she hung onto my back while swimming, she whispered in my ear, "Can I come and live with you? I need a home." I turned to look at her and, smiling, said, "Of course!" We took Brittany home that night, and she has lived with us ever since. Within a year, we adopted her and settled in as a family of six.

One year after adopting Brittany, I began to feel restless in my faith. This discontentment in my faith scared me. As I continued teaching the visually impaired, I desired to make an impact in the public schools where I taught, so I went on a crusade to start after-school staff prayer groups. In a short time, the Lord was graciously moving the hearts of the teachers to form prayer groups. Every fall, new prayer groups started before or after school. During these times, the teachers were able to pray together and share their burdens.

Even though the prayer groups were a tremendous blessing, my life mimicked that of a hummingbird as I found myself fluttering from one cause to another. My daughter stated one sunny day, "Mom, you are the boldest person I know!" Unsure whether or not that was a compliment, I forged ahead by initiating Bible clubs in our local schools. I was completely unaware that God was going to use my unpolished character traits to accomplish His will in even greater areas.

Two years passed, and family life became scheduled and routine. The feeling of restlessness began to seep more deeply into my heart. This increasing restlessness and discontentment became troublesome to me.

Surprisingly, the desire to parent more children began to resurface. At first, I wondered if I was going through some life-altering season. Trying to ignore the ignited spark, I quenched the thought by stuffing it down in the recesses of my heart. "Anyway," I thought, "people would think I was absurd. Seeking to raise more children at my age of 44 is crazy!" Standing at the sink one sunny, summer day, I prayed that the Lord would snuff out this flame of desire. "At this stage in my life, I should be sitting back and enjoying family and friends. And why am I not content with four children?" The following day, I read this verse from the Bible,

4

"Give justice to the weak and the fatherless; maintain the right of the afflicted and the destitute. Rescue the weak and the needy; deliver them from the hand of the wicked" (Ps. 82:3-4).

A sense of relief washed over me as I discovered that the Lord was leading our family in a new direction. Kerry and I felt we had more to give as parents, so the next logical step was to embark on the path of becoming foster parents. We began by taking classes. During this time, I sat in church one Sunday night and listened to a missionary from Zambia. I asked myself, "Where in the world is Zambia anyway?" After examining a map of Africa, I discovered it was a landlocked country near Southern Africa. I realized that I knew nothing about the country. Setting my poor geography skills aside, I was moved with compassion as he explained that his ministry focused on one particular village, Baluba. It contained three hundred fifty orphans, and more than half of the children were in need of sponsorship in order to meet their basic needs. With Christmas just one week away, I thought it was important for my daughters to extend their kindness to others who were less fortunate.

After the service, we quickly exited the chapel to select the picture of the orphan girl we wanted to sponsor. I was overwhelmed at the sight of a board filled with pictures of desolate children who were all underweight, with tattered clothing hanging loosely over their gaunt shoulders. I found my eyes drawn to a young, thirteen-year-old girl wearing a too-large school uniform and worn-out black shoes. I snatched up the card, completely unaware of the adventure that awaited us. Little did we realize that when we began sponsoring Victoria Chisanga, orphan number Z0063001, our lives would soon interlock across the world!

Victoria was a beautiful, young teenager with a chocolate brown complexion and deep, brown eyes. She had endured more hardship than most high school students her age; yet, surprisingly, her heartaches were managed with extraordinary grace and quietness of spirit. Victoria's contagious smile revealed her charming dimples. Her slender frame added charm to her spirited personality.

Raised as an only child, Victoria lost her mother in childbirth. In Zambia, the mortality rate is so high that one out of every four children is parentless.

Victoria was a vivacious child. After the death of her mother she was raised by her father, Charles. The two of them lived in Lusaka, the capital city of Zambia. The country has an unemployment rate of 75 percent, yet, remarkably, her father was one of those precious few who had a coveted job. He worked at a local meat market, which allowed him to bring meat home every night. This provided a precious source of protein, a rare commodity, considering the circumstances in the village in which they lived. Even though they lived in a village in the capital city without running water or electricity, Victoria's basic needs were met.

> Average life-expectancy at birth is 38.6 years in Zambia.

Victoria was the apple of her father's eye. One dark day when Victoria was at the tender age of six, her father came home from work ill. Malaria had struck again. This disease is usually treatable, but, in parts of the world where there is a lack of funds for medication, this disease is deadly. He was buried the next day. This young child now faced despair on every side. Victoria was without a mother and a father—truly a double orphan. Despite these unspeakable tragedies, Victoria coped with amazing resilience and bravery. Victoria Chisanga joined the ranks of the throngs of orphans.

Victoria's grandmother and grandfather now became her caretakers. Her grandmother was a woman of dignity with a shining smile. Her tall and slender frame was accented by her handcrafted dress, which fit perfectly, and by her long, carefully braided hair. Grandfather was a tall and handsome man, but he lost his job at the local supermarket in the capital city. Their faith in God was their anchor amidst the storms of excruciating hardships.

With both parents gone, Victoria moved into the village with her grandparents. She was abruptly faced with the harsh reality of poverty in the village and the serious hardships that go along with it. This village was a destitute and disturbing place, lacking running water and electricity. Walking miles to school in the Zambian sun was only the beginning of many trials she would face. The school system desperately lacked funds, supplies, food, or textbooks. There was only a slate chalkboard for the teachers to use, and the curriculum was years behind the American school system. Their school uniforms were a basic blue; short hair was mandatory, and the girls couldn't wear braids, jewelry, or anything that might make them different from one another or even remotely attractive to the young, male teachers.

The male teachers were taskmasters, quick to administer corporal punishment by beating students with a pipe or stick at the slightest provocation. Children walked miles to school and frequently arrived a few minutes late, resulting in severe corporal punishment. Missing an assignment or talking in class would evoke anger from their teacher. Victoria, even though compliant by nature, was beaten for whispering to a friend. If she arrived a few minutes late to school because she was taking care of an ailing grandmother, the taskmaster would bring her to the front of the class and strike her with a pipe. Victoria did not question or challenge authority and had learned to accept these conditions as part of her daily life. Even though Victoria went to great lengths to obey every rule, she was subject to the ruthless schoolmasters who showed no mercy.

Village life was a harsh reality, with none of the creature comforts we take for granted here in America. Hauling water, preparing sparse meals over an open fire, and working in the cornfields developed an inner strength and poise in Victoria. She did not have any shoes to wear as she toiled in the hot sun. Rather than complain, she was thankful that her grandparents cared enough to take her into their home. As a result, she faced each day with courage and dignity.

On the other side of the world, the Frantz family continued to sponsor Victoria in order to provide her basic needs, including education and food. The letters and dialogue between us started to bridge the gap, and we formed a cordial relationship. Our family soon discovered that Victoria's village life was filled with challenges and difficulties. Each month I would send letters and small trinkets to encourage Victoria to persevere amidst her difficult circumstances. One summer day in 2010, I was pleasantly surprised to receive a letter from Victoria. Sitting on my comfortable couch with a warm cup of coffee, I picked it up and began to read. The letter depicted Victoria's harsh life in the village along with the status of her ailing grandmother. Part of the letter read:

"Hello Frantz Family, greetings from our Lord and Savior Jesus Christ. I am Victoria Chisanga (orphan number Z0063001) and I live in Baluba Village. I am thirteen years old. I have to walk five kilometers to school every day. I get good grades and study very hard. My mom died when I was born and my dad died when I was six. I live in Baluba Village, Zambia with my grandmother and grandfather. They are both ill and I take care of them.

In the Name of Jesus Christ, Victoria Chisanga."

I read the letter over and over, trying to understand the gravity of her circumstances. As I mulled over her words, a verse came to mind. "Religion that God our Father accepts as pure and faultless is this: to look after orphans and widows in their distress and to keep oneself from being polluted by the world" (James 1:27). As I held the letter, tears ran down my cheek, and I knew where the Lord was leading our family; I was being led to adopt thirteen-year-old Victoria Chisanga! I realized that the Lord was "the Father to the fatherless," and He was calling me to take care of His child.

The next challenge would be to inform my husband that I wanted to adopt a teenager from the other side of the world. When Kerry came home from a busy day of pastoring at Grace Presbyterian Church in Peoria, I wanted to capture the right moment to approach the topic of adoption. As I set dishes in the sink I tried to be as casual as possible. I turned toward Kerry and nonchalantly stated, "Could you read this letter from Victoria because I feel that we should adopt her." Nothing stops my husband in his tracks, but this time he immediately turned and looked at me with a stunned expression. We sat down at the kitchen table, and I reread the letter from Victoria. After a prayer and heartfelt discussion, Kerry was also convinced that we should start the adoption process.

The next morning, I sat nervously with a phone in my hand, vocally rehearsing how to approach the topic of adoption with the administrator of the sponsoring organization, IN Network. My strong-willed personality gave me the boldness I needed to proceed with the phone call. I quickly dialed the number. "Hello, my name is Nancy Frantz," I stated matter-of-factly, "and we sponsor Victoria Chisanga, orphan number Z0063001. My husband and I would like to adopt her." There was a long silence that felt like eternity before the administrator flatly responded, "In the history of our organization, no one has ever asked to adopt a sponsored child." Leave it to me to be the rebel with a cause!

Dialogue and correspondence began between our family and the pastors in Zambia. Pastor Bernard, an advocate for the needs of the orphans in Baluba, is a small man in stature with a handsome smile. He is a quiet and meek man with a deep faith and a heart for helping orphans. Realizing that he had to broach the topic of adoption with Victoria and her grandparents, Pastor Bernard traveled to the remote Baluba Village to explain to them that a couple in America wanted to adopt her. America, the land of plenty, is a coveted place to live from the perspective of the Zambians.

Victoria sat quietly on the bed with her grandmother as the pastor explained the opportunities that awaited her in America. Victoria's grandmother depended on Victoria to take care of her, but the love she had for her granddaughter exceeded her own needs.

Victoria was excited about having new parents and having her needs met. On the other hand, she had to grapple with the thought of leaving her ailing grandmother. Victoria's grandmother, a woman of great faith and dependence on God, daily encouraged her by saying that God had chosen her to go to America.

Victoria also had to face her fears of becoming part of a new family and trying to fit into American society. She had never even seen a picture of America, much less lived

> According to the Zambian Adoption Act, prospective adoptive parents must foster a child in Zambia for six months.

there! But she also realized her intense suffering would end once she was adopted into our family. A decision was made, and Victoria agreed to the adoption. She penned a letter to the US, stating her desire to be adopted.

Amazingly, God was preparing her heart along with ours to hopefully be part of the Frantz family.

We began to make overtures to adopt Victoria, which involved a lengthy and tedious process. Reams of paperwork and affidavits were drafted; we began to take class after class to fulfill the US regulations for international adoption. Home visits with social workers and extra classes were needed, due to Victoria's age. Since she had just turned thirteen, officials red-flagged our paperwork, in fear that our intention for adopting her would be for sex trafficking.

Adoption of older international children was rare in the US. Consequently, Catholic Social Services requested that Kerry and I take a daylong class in Illinois to fulfill the extra requirements. When I inquired about the cost of the class, a representative blankly replied, "The one-day class will cost you two thousand dollars."

I gasped and said, "You are kidding, aren't you?"

"No," the representative retorted.

"Can I make you a deal?" I quickly replied. "Can I compensate you one thousand dollars for the one-day class, and then I will donate the other thousand dollars toward food for the orphans in the village?"

"No, we need the two thousand dollar payment today."

I shook my head in disbelief, and as I wrote out the check, I was reminded of the verse ". . . a bribe corrupts the heart" (Ecc. 7:7).

Due to corruption in Zambia, red tape stretched from America to Victoria's homeland. Zambia does not have governmental regulations or guidelines for adoption; therefore, in 2010, only a meager eight adoptions out of a vast one-and-a-half-million orphans occurred. We were pioneering new governmental ground, and I wondered how the Frantz family could contribute to one ninth of the total adoptions in 2011. The odds were insurmountable! At the end of many exhausting days of working through a maze of paperwork, I would lay in bed awake, worrying if we would ever be able to adopt a child from Zambia. Was I ready to leave my comfortable lifestyle and permanently change our family dynamics? Even though we were assured that the Lord was calling us to go to Zambia, my faith wavered, and I struggled to believe that God could do the impossible. Questions plagued me as we forged ahead with the adoption: "Who am I, to be called to such an overwhelming mission? Am I strong enough to endure the journey?" I had to lean on Him to equip me for the overwhelming task ahead.

Meanwhile, Victoria had begun to embrace the idea of adoption and started pondering an uncertain future. Both Victoria and her grandmother did not have any information about life in America.

Victoria shared how she felt about the adoption. "When I was at school, one of the volunteers of the orphan organization told me that a sponsor wanted to adopt me! When I heard that, I was really scared because I did not know what was going on and how Mr. and Mrs. Frantz would treat me in their new country. One of my biggest fears was my English and how I would communicate; how was I going to adjust to my new home, new school and family? I was worried about my grandmother, who had a stroke, as I took care of her through the night. On the other hand, I knew that being adopted and living in America was going to change my life. I thought that maybe someday after I went to college, I would take care of my grandparents. My life in the village was not that good, but I was really thankful with the little I had since I knew that my grandparents did not have enough money to buy everything I needed in life. Although we struggled, my grandmother was a strong Christian and she taught me the Bible. The good news was that my new family is Christian and I knew I would be safe. When I was in Zambia, I began to dream about living in America."

Victoria, age 12, walking 5K to school

Chapter 2
Two for the Price of One

One hot and humid night my husband became frustrated with the arduous adoption process as he realized that we were in it for the long haul. With all the effort and expense of the adoption, Kerry wanted to double his efforts. It seemed logical to him that since we were already going to have to navigate the Zambian courts, we might as well adopt an orphaned Zambian boy along with Victoria. A total of four girls in the Frantz home was not Kerry's idea of fun. "Why not?" he thought, since the process had already been arduous and costly. Besides, Kerry is so competitive he wanted to be able to field a baseball team, and he was determined to develop a star athlete. I laughed at the prospect of having six children and moaned at the thought of middle age encroaching.

Throwing all hesitation to the wind, I quickly warmed up to the proposal. This meant another phone call to IN Network. I felt a little braver when I made the second phone call. When I spoke to an administrator I stated that Kerry and I would also like to adopt a boy. Again there was a long silence on the phone. "We will dialogue with Pastor Bernard and get his input," the administrator said, after a stunned response. Pastor Bernard quickly jumped on board, knowing that a nurturing home would benefit another orphan. As a result, a plan was formed that involved a team consisting of Pastor Bernard and his wife, Medica, along with administrators representing IN Network.

Their mission was to go to Baluba and find an orphaned boy who was in the most desperate situation. Knowing the gravity of the decision and selection process, our family prayed and fasted throughout the day.

In the middle of the night of September 15, 2010, I tossed and turned, knowing that our quiet life would quickly change with additional children. Unable to sleep, I raced downstairs to check our email to see if a child had been selected. I clicked on the email from Pastor Bernard that had arrived in the middle of the night. It stated that the team had completed their mission. When I began to read it, my mouth dropped open. Sitting on the edge of the chair I rubbed my eyes and scratched my head, wondering if I had misread the message. Again, scanning the email, my eyes focused on the word "boys." Unbelievably, a set of twin boys was chosen! Even though their age was undetermined, their age range was guessed to be between eight to ten years old. Their names were Andrew and Andre Mumba. We were getting a two for one deal!

They were double orphans with both parents deceased and living in the most destitute poverty. I sat in front of the computer screen, stunned, trying to wrap my mind around three additional children entering the Frantz home. The boys were so young, and I was not a spring chicken. My two older children were already starting to sprout their wings. Would I be able to raise a second batch of children? Fully awake, I raced upstairs to inform my husband, who had instigated the boy's adoption. "You will soon be a new dad of twin boys who are about ten," I announced, jumping onto the bed. Startled out of his sleep, a laugh of unbelief bellowed from my husband.

Kerry, having finally found the fielders for his team, was excited at the prospect of quick-footed Zambian boys. We both lay in bed staring at the ceiling, thinking that we were both crazy and exhibiting a midlife crisis.

Even though Andrew and Andre had grown up in the same village as Victoria, they led different lives. The boys rarely attended school and did not know how to read or write. They were village street kids, wandering the grimy paths in search for food. One desperate day, without food, they stole a mango off a tree, and police were called to the village to punish the boys. They were severely beaten for the incident. At times their grandmother would use an old high heeled shoe and have the boys place their hands flat on the ground. Then she would proceed to pound the heel into their hands and feet. Life had become unbearable for Andrew and Andre.

In the village, Andre and Andrew had a bad reputation for fighting other children. Since they did not have any parental guidance, it was survival of the fittest. The twins were inseparable, trying to gather strength to live another day. Life was unforgiving.

> A strong argument could be made that the twin boys chosen to come to America caused the greatest disturbance in the village. Most children pursuing international dreams must rise to the top of their class; whereas these boys demonstrated that God would use the most destitute of this world to show His great wisdom.

Their grandmother and Pastor Bernard thought that they were between eight and eleven years old. Therefore, the lawyer declared them to be eleven. Astoundingly, they had the weight of a three-year-old, a measly forty pounds. Pictures were sent to us, and their plight was evident. With ribs showing, grimacing faces, torn clothing, the desperation shown in their eyes. Their bodies revealed a life of suffering. In the picture, they stood shoeless on the hot gravel. Again, Pastor Bernard went into their village to consult with their now bedridden grandmother to get her consent for their pending adoption.

Due to AIDS, their grandmother was suffering immensely and losing the battle against the deadly disease. Being relieved at no longer having to be the boys' caretaker, she readily agreed to the adoption. Just like Victoria, the boys had no knowledge of and had never seen a picture of America. However, their grandmother agreed that anything would be better than starvation. The adoption for the three children was quickly set into motion.

We soon learned that corruption was entrenched in the Zambian infrastructure. Money transfers of thousands of dollars became a common demand from the social worker and court officials. The more funds that were transferred the more demanding the officials became. Even though Kerry and I were exasperated by the adoption process, it paled in comparison to the suffering we knew that Andrew, Andre, and Victoria endured. In the middle of the night on January 30, I checked our email, and there was the news we had been long waiting for. The court date in Zambia was finally set for February 2011.

We were assured that the Lord was calling us to go to Zambia, and we had to lean on Him to equip us for the insurmountable task that lay ahead. Having only a few days to prepare for the trip, we frantically packed extra clothes for the children and supplies for the pastor and his family and then anxiously waited to meet the children for the first time.

The night before we left, when everyone was asleep, I sat quietly in the dark living room with the luggage neatly lined up against the wall. I shook my head in disbelief, not knowing where our journey would lead us. I knew Kerry and I had stepped out of the boundaries of what was normal and could easily appear foolish to those looking into our lives. Was I strong enough to travel down the road of foreign adoption?

I tried to shake the feelings of doubt that surfaced like dark shadows on the wall. My strong will that drove my passion to adopt the children began to crumble, and fear seeped into my soul. After a year of pressing forward with paperwork and jumping over obstacles, I was now weak and vulnerable. There was nothing left. In the dark, I bowed my head, with tears streaming down my face, and prayed for mercy. I was reminded of a verse that led me down the path of adoption: "He raises the poor from the dust and lifts the needy from the ash heap; He seats them with the princes, with the princes of their people" (Ps. 113:7).

Andre, approximately age 9, in the village

Andrew's sponsorship picture at age 9

Chapter 3
Village Life to Civilization

We discovered that Zambia is one of the African countries hardest hit by AIDS. Close to twenty percent of children, or slightly over one million, are orphans. Approximately seventy percent of the population earns less than one dollar per day. Older siblings are often forced to drop out of the educational system in order to care for their younger siblings.

As we continued the adoption process, we became discouraged by the corruption that infiltrated the government. Zambia is void of any adoption agencies due to the lack of resources and infrastructure. Without aid from an adoption agency, finding housing, transportation, and food near the children's remote village was nearly impossible.

Fortunately, as we neared our departure date, I received information about a missionary family in Ndola, a town close to Baluba Village. Teri and David had lived in Zambia for eight years. They graciously helped us find housing and became an active part of the adoption process. As soon as we walked on Zambian soil, we began to realize that the Lord had a divine plan and that Teri and David were involved in the process.

The culture was extremely difficult to navigate. We flew into Ndola, which is one of the largest towns in Zambia. The airport consisted of a small runway with a barbed wire fence surrounding a small white building. Fences were high, armed guards were alert, and officials were suspicious of Americans who travel to Zambia. Teri Wilson greeted us at the airport with a cordial handshake. Teri, a tall slender woman with a sincere and gracious smile, ushered us into her van. She too struggled to survive the oppressive culture, but her quiet demeanor immediately put us at ease.

As we were pulling out of the airport, several servicemen ran to our car window, heckling about a tip she gave to another porter.

Gently she reassured them that she had given a tip to other workers and quietly drove away.

Next, her mission was to find housing for our small family. We navigated around potholes that were the size of elephants, driving past shanty villages with acacia trees that gracefully adorned the vast grasslands. The culture soon began to capture my heart, and I felt a sense of peace. I was amazed at the vast number of Zambian people walking along dirt roads. Mamas carried babies on their backs as they walked briskly along the busy road.

As we turned around the bend, we arrived at another missionary's guesthouse owned by Dan and Amanda West. The house was surrounded by wired fence with glass embedded in the top of cement blocks, and armed guards were assigned to open the gate. Kerry and I had no idea how blessed we were to have the support of the missionaries because there were no known hotels in Ndola. The modest guesthouse was perfect, and we had the luxury of running water and electricity. After an exhausting day and a twenty-five-hour flight, we were thankful to have landed safely on Zambian soil.

That night the sky was clear, and the stars were brilliant. Kerry and I sat quietly on a cement block, contemplating the gravity of adopting three additional children. Do we have the energy needed to raise a set of twin boys? How will we be able to handle three international children in our home? And whose idea was this anyway? These were questions that plagued us. We then slid under the mosquito netting, anxiously waiting to meet the children in the morning.

When we awoke to the roosters crowing, we realized this was the long awaited day. It was a sleepless night mingled with hopes and fears, anxiety and anticipation. Nervously, we prepared to meet the three children in the village. I packed trinkets for the other children and granola bars for Andrew, Andre, and Victoria. Pastor Bernard and his wife Medica escorted us to the village and helped translate. Pastor Bernard was an advocate for the Baluba village and cared for the orphans.

Dressed in an exquisite African dress, Medica, a mother of five children, was adorned in teal and gold. A woman of faith and inner strength, Medica encouraged me during the long drive to the village. She had an infectious laugh that put me at ease. Pastor Bernard was a humble man with a good sense of humor.

As we drove through the rocky narrow roads to find the remote village, I realized we were in very primitive surroundings. Billiant, a tall quiet man who worked as a mechanic and driver for IN Network, also escorted us. Billiant had five small children and had grown up in a similar village himself. As such, he understood their plight.

Teri was a continual support by giving up her time and vehicle. She had a quiet and sweet presence as she drove us to the Baluba village. As the six of us traveled to the village, Bernard helped navigate through the winding roads.

I sat quietly in the car and wondered if I would recognize the children from their sponsorship pictures. I was ready to meet the children and longed for them to become part of our family. A sweet calmness swept over me like a cool mist on a hot summer day.

I held their picture in my hand, which showed the boys wearing large tattered shirts that draped over their frail bodies, their arms hanging limp at their sides. Andre and Andrew were barefoot and did not have shoes. Andrew and Andre were unable to attend school due to their lack of shoes. Deep suffering was etched on their faces.

Victoria's picture was similar—she was dressed in a plain blue school uniform that hung at her shoulders. Her hair was cut short, which was mandatory for attending school due to an epidemic of lice in the village.

When we drove into the village I suddenly realized I had stepped back in time. There were no signs of any motor vehicles, lights, or modern conveniences. I was surrounded by stunted trees that dotted a barren landscape. In the dark crevasses of the hillside wild dogs roamed in the shadows. Grass huts were scattered along the countryside, and I knew that one of the vast number of shanties was the home of Andrew and Andre Mumba. We stopped on the side of the dirt road as we parked adjacent to their hut. Everyone in the vehicle was silent, taking in the living condition of the boys. I stepped out of the sedan and timidly walked around a bend in the dirt road. Dust huddled around my legs. Next to a small garden planted in the dry ground was a small thatched hut.

Standing before me were two small boys in frayed, threadbare, faded blue school uniforms. Shyly they greeted me with a handshake and timid smile; neither Andre nor Andrew spoke English. Andrew and Andre were smaller than an average American six-year-old. As their slight arms reached out to greet us, I noticed that their ankles were the size of thin branches. I bent down and hugged them, patting their round bellies to reassure the boys of our care for them. I was initially relieved to hear they had received our support and had eaten balanced meals. However, as I scanned my surroundings, I quickly realized there was no food around or in the hut and deduced that the funds for the food did not reach their mouths.

Shockingly, I realized that the boys' extended bellies were due to malnutrition. At that moment, I thought back to the time I viewed a humanitarian organization's television commercial pleading for money that showed starving African children. Sitting comfortably on the couch and eating a bowl of popcorn I easily discarded any feeling of guilt. But now it was a memory I could hardly bear; the moment seemed surreal. I could not believe that I was standing next to starving boys in Africa, who we were trying to adopt.

Before I could fully grasp the gravity of the situation we were quickly ushered into their grandmother's hut. Kerry and I were greeted by the boys' aunt and her six children. When we entered the meager two-room hut, my mind still could not comprehend the magnitude of their poverty. Without electricity and ventilation, it was dark and musty. The grandmother lay on a mattress in the corner, obviously too sick to take care of the twins.

The roof appeared to be a checkerboard of sticks crisscrossing each other. The flimsy beams sagged from the weight of the brush lying on top, appearing as though it would cave in during the next rainy season. The cousins and relatives gathered in the small stifling room and sat in front of the mattress. The family matriarch sat in the center of the mattress. The air was musty, and, even though it was a bright sunny day, the room was dark. Caucasians were a rare sight in the village and the family's eyes were fixed on Kerry and me.

Zambians are formal in their greetings and politeness is highly respected. Children are to bow one knee or curtsy as they shake an adult's hand. The boys had been groomed to be on their best behavior to advance to the land of plenty (America).

I scanned the room again and failed to find any food. A sick child lay curled up in the middle of the floor without any blankets or comfort to ease his suffering. A small window let in a glimpse of light, but could not illuminate the gloom that permeated the room. I began to understand the intense suffering the boys had endured. Although eight children lived in the small hut, there was no evidence of extra clothing, personal belongings, food, or water. Andrew and Andre were the only ones in the household wearing flip flops. The rest of the family was barefoot, enduring the hot dusty roads with no foot protection.

Moved by their suffering, I gave everything I had brought for the children. Unfortunately, without prior knowledge of how desperate conditions were, I quickly realized that I should have also brought food. My heart ached to fill their bellies.

Pastor Bernard translated as we spoke with the grandmother. She expressed that her health was failing and understood the boys needed a home; therefore, she gave us her blessing to adopt them.

Then the twins ushered us to an adjacent room and showed us where they slept with other family members. Andrew and Andre were assigned to sleep in the corner of the room. They proudly showed us their personal space in the small room. There were not any blankets, pillows, or beds, just a bare corner. At night when it rained, the boys would stand in the corner to keep from getting wet. When the temperatures dipped down into the fifties at night, they would huddle together on the cement floor for warmth. These were normal conditions for the boys.

As we began to leave, the boys hugged their grandmother goodbye. Unbelievably, without hesitation or question, Andrew and Andre left with us, never looking back. They would never step foot into their hut again; they were saying good-bye, not just to the suffering and hardship but to the only family they ever knew. Andrew and Andre appeared to be relieved to have parents who were able to care for them. Any fears of strange Caucasian American parents were quickly snuffed out by the thoughts of food, family, and nurturing. They had nothing to bring with them, not even a toothbrush. All they owned were the clothes on their backs.

As we traveled down the windy dusty path to Victoria's hut, the boys walked hand in hand. They were content to have each other. The air was hot and heavy with the sun beating down on our heads. The narrow path wound around the wooded field, and tall grass surrounding the path swirled around the boys, as a gentle breeze swept across the path. After walking for fifteen minutes we finally rounded a bend. There before me was a small hut. The humble dwelling was surrounded by lush corn and a vegetable garden. Victoria's grandmother was a resourceful woman, finding ways to stretch her food supply.

Out of the hut came a tall and elegant woman with open arms running toward me. Her warm smile immediately put me at ease. After greeting me with a warm embrace, she profusely thanked me for adopting Victoria. Her harsh life of endless poverty was chiseled in the lines of her face. Long braids framed her shoulders, and her dress was finely embroidered.

Victoria's grandmother smiled from ear to ear, thanking God for our intervention in Victoria's life. Behind her was a tall, slender girl, who shyly and slowly approached us. Victoria wore an African dress woven with bright colors which fitted her frail frame. The bright colors were sewn into the weave of her tribal design. Victoria was a symbol of refinement amongst poverty, a rare jewel found in Baluba Village. We had waited three years for this moment. Before me stood the young girl who I had prayed for year after year, day after day. I looked into her eyes and saw her sweet smile; I felt compelled to hug her as I tried to reassure her of our love.

Victoria's thoughts when we first met:

"The first time I saw Nancy and Kerry Frantz, it was kind of scary because I thought it was the last time I would be able to spend time with my grandparents and friends. I was a little nervous, too, because I was getting a new dad, mom, and new little brothers; but the thought of a new family made me feel happy too."

Only 22% of Zambia's total population currently has access to electricity.

We then entered Victoria's hut. It was a small two room structure with her bed in the front room. Surprisingly, Victoria had pictures of our family hanging on the wall above her bed. There we were, the Frantz family, displayed on the plastered wall. Victoria's tall, slender grandfather stood quietly in the corner of the room. He leaned up against a water jug, which was their meager supply of water. We sat down on a small bench across from Victoria who was sitting on her bed. Victoria shyly smiled, showing her dimples. Her grandmother, who spoke fluent English, related that Victoria's biological father and mother had died. Her mother during childbirth and malaria had taken her father's life when Victoria was six years old.

I did not want to leave without confirmation from Victoria that she was certain she wanted to be adopted. Looking straight into Victoria's eyes, I addressed her quietly. "Victoria, do you still want to come to America and be part of the Frantz family?"

Everyone gazed at Victoria as silence permeated the walls of the hut. I sat on the edge of the chair, afraid to breathe. Like sand slipping through the narrow passage of an hourglass, time stood still. Victoria gazed into my eyes as she whispered, with a smile on her face, "Yes, I would like that very much." Victoria's name was engraved not only in my heart but also in the heart of God. A rush of relief washed over me as I realized we were one step closer to adopting Victoria.

We hugged each other and said our long goodbyes. When we exited Victoria's humble abode, she was never to enter the doorway again. Victoria was entering another doorway that led beyond what she could ever have envisioned. As I turned and looked back, I saw a small thatched outhouse in the back of her home. I realized that America would hold many changes for the three children. When Andrew and Andre left the village, they did not have a teddy bear or blanket to bring with them for comfort or a keepsake. Victoria also walked out of her hut with empty arms.

Amazingly, the kids quickly slid into the car and willingly went with us. The twins had never been in a car. It was like they were on their first rollercoaster ride. The boys peered out the back window with wide eyes and mouths gaped open. Their heads bobbed up and down as they quietly chatted to each other in the Bemba language, excited to be passengers in a vehicle. They were like perched birds fascinated by their surroundings. They were leaving the village for the first time in their lives.

I glanced into the backseat and noticed Victoria resting her head against the seat, tears running down her face. Victoria contemplated her grandmother's well-being now that she would be gone. She wondered who would take care of her in the middle of the night. At thirteen years of age, she was able to comprehend the implications of the adoption. I reached back and held her hand. I tried to reassure Victoria that, even though she was mourning the loss of her grandmother, she would be all right.

The children were beaming with excitement as we drove up to the guesthouse. The armed guard quickly ushered us in. Dan and Amanda, missionaries with three small children, lived in the same compound and were in charge of renting out the small guesthouse. As we entered the guesthouse, the children immediately tried to take in their new surroundings. They were ecstatic to have running water and electricity.

The first priority was to teach the children how to use the toilet. The concept of water swirling around a porcelain bowl was comical to the boys. To our relief, Pastor Bernard intervened and helped them learn to use the bathroom. What was a seemingly simple task became an ordeal. When do you put the lid up or down? Do you stand or sit? What is toilet paper used for? These were questions we had to address. According to the boys, standing on the stool over the hole seemed the most convenient to them. It made sense since they always stood over a hole in their outhouse in the village.

> Parasitic worms are mostly due to contaminated water sources.

The next priority was bath time. Never having taken a bath or even having running water set us up for a tub adventure and it was a fascinating ordeal. After scrubbing and scrubbing with plenty of play time in ice cold water, I finally drained the tub. The bottom of the tub was black; and at first I didn't know if it was dirt, slime or some other unidentified matter. I washed out the tub with my hands, accidently splashing the water up into my face. Later I realized that the unidentified substance was actually worms, thousands of them. The lousy varmints were everywhere! Worms came out of their scalp and were peering out of their noses. It

> Preventative medication in Zambia for worms or malaria is not an option for Zambian families. Each live on just enough food for the day.

was quite a treat! The mystery was solved as to why the boys were eating as much as a two-hundred-pound man when I cooked for them.

Since the boys had never been treated for worms, they had a severe case, which resulted in the bulging bellies. Victoria, with her playful sense of humor, said, "The worms especially like the sausage you cook. Look at the two pounds of sausage the boys have eaten in order to feed the worms!" The worms apparently were hungry too. In severe cases, the worms will come out through the nose, mouth, or the stool. What would a day in Zambia be like without malaria or worms? The worms saw their final days as I treated the boys with deworming pills. The medicine would fend off the worms for six months.

Following the bathroom fun, Medica, who cared for the village orphans, snagged up their torn and tattered uniforms so that other children in the village could wear them. The boys proudly wore their new shorts and shirts and strutted across the room with their new gym shoes.

A basic hygiene practice such as brushing teeth was a completely foreign practice for the children. Putting toothpaste on a toothbrush and then running the water over it was an activity that prompted the boys to splash water everywhere. Gagging from swallowing the toothpaste and chomping on the bristles made the boys appear as mad men foaming at the mouth.

Afterwards, I turned my attention to Victoria, who was closely watching the bathroom fun. I took Victoria into the bedroom to give her the clothes I had brought from America. She sat meekly on the edge of the bed with her hands on her knees, excited to try on her clothes. When she tried on a skirt she twirled and danced like a ballerina. Victoria thought it was the greatest number of outfits she had ever laid her eyes on. They fit her beautifully. It was more than she could have imagined. At the bottom of the suitcase were basic tan shoes with a thin strap. Victoria slipped her feet into them and her face lit up with a smile that would melt any mother's heart. They fit and would protect her feet from the rough terrain, taking her another step away from the destitution of the village. Victoria began to feel like a lovely young lady.

Later, as the boys played in the small cement courtyard, Kerry attempted to play catch with them. When the ball was tossed to the boys, they were unable to catch it and the ball dropped to the ground. I knew what Kerry was thinking; his thoughts were like the transparent window pane I was looking through. His anticipation of training star athletes quickly diminished. Suddenly, and without warning, a dog came pouncing from nowhere and began to chase Andrew. Panicking, Andrew frantically ran toward the guesthouse. As he looked behind at the ferocious dog, he collided with the strong rebar windows. Blood spilled down his face and splattered on his shirt; a look of fear was imbedded on his face. We promptly cleaned him up and hugged him as an assurance of our love and protection.

After a long day, I tucked the twins into one small bed. Mosquito netting framed the boys as they lay on their bed, wearing their first pair of underwear and pajamas. Suddenly, I heard sweet voices harmonizing with each other as Andrew and Andre sang tribal songs. The sounds of their voices were like angels singing. Never having had toys, Andrew and Andre hugged their stuffed animals like precious treasures. As they lay on their bed for the first time, I marveled at their contentment and sensed that they felt safe and secure.

Exhausted, late that night I sat on the edge of my bed with the mosquito netting softly flowing from the breeze coming through an open window. I contemplated the journey of faith the Lord had led us on. Here we were in a guesthouse across the world with three children we had known for less than one day and who would one day become our children. Andrew, Andre, and Victoria may become part of our family. Amazingly, I realized that I loved them as I did my own biological children. God began to show me His unconditional love for His orphans.

I struggled with jet lag, and the impact of taking care of three new children immediately sent me into overdrive. The next morning my mind was in a fog and I tried to collect my thoughts as I processed the midlife change I encountered. As I scrambled out of bed, I was keenly aware that the children needed guidance. I heard the sound of a chair scraping on the floor, and it dawned on me that the children were already up. When I turned the corner and peered into the kitchen, the three of them were quietly sitting at the table with hands folded staring at each other, unsure of what to expect. It was obvious that they had one question on their mind: would there be food to eat?

I asked how long they had been sitting there, and Victoria quietly said, "We have been up since sunrise (five a.m.) but didn't know what to do."

I knew that it was important for the children to understand that food would always be available to them. I quickly scrambled around the kitchen to cook the brown eggs we obtained from the open air market.

The next two days were quite an adventure as I tried to teach them how to use modern conveniences. Never having had electricity meant light switches that were turned on and off a hundred times a day. Running water was absent from their homes; therefore, water faucets were turned on but rarely turned off. A hut without appliances meant burners were now played with and left on. Dealing with their curiosity caused me to contemplate the vast differences between village life and American culture. Andrew, Andre and Victoria had never tasted ice or enjoyed a cool beverage from a refrigerator. They had never put their head on a pillow, hugged a favorite blanket, or had light at night to read by. Kerry and I wanted to show that we cared for them by providing for their basic needs.

It was hard to imagine a life that did not include watching a television show, taking a hot shower, or feeling the refreshment of air conditioning. Having a cabinet full of food or tasting the delicacy of ice cream was never a reality for these children. The simple task of tucking them into bed gave them assurance that their needs would be provided for.

Every day brought more obstacles, as I was uninformed about dietary issues. Preparing food became another hurdle. Cooked poultry and rice-based dishes were easy on the children's digestive system. Never before having had chocolate, ice cream, bakery items, chips, sugared drinks, milk, juice, or other basic items caused their digestive system to go into overdrive. The children ate more than most men and would sit quietly at the table until I asked if they wanted a second helping. As a result of my satisfying their ferocious appetites, happiness was in the air. At six a.m. every day, Victoria would ask daily what was for dinner. Meat is a delicacy in Zambia, and Victoria would anxiously wait for dinner in order to consume as much meat as possible. The children lacked protein, and their bodies craved basic nutrition.

At the end of the day, we asked the children what the highlight of their day was, and each of them said, "Eating."

We soon realized that the twin boys were quite different in personalities. Andrew was more talkative and expressive, learned quickly, and loved to laugh. Andre was more serious and quiet, and had a sweet disposition. Even though Andre was an inch taller than Andrew, he weighed less than forty pounds. Andre longed to have a family and dreamt of one day becoming a soldier. Back in the village he often played in the dirt, pretending to be a courageous man. Andre was less aware of time and what the future held for him. By contrast, Andrew smiled at the slightest delight, even though his body craved food. He was more talkative with the other children in the village and enjoyed playing soccer by using corn stocks as a ball.

> Abuse of children is encouraged and socially accepted in Zambian culture. Children are problems to be fixed and not gifts to be treasured.

In Zambia, Andre was considered the "weaker" twin; therefore, he was mistreated more often and fed less. Zambians commonly believe that, when twins are born, the second child is demon possessed. Sadly, the second-born twin would often be killed. Thankfully, Andre survived. Even though both boys suffered in the village, he endured the harsher treatment. Every day in the village meant a day of rigorous work in order to survive. Since the age of four, Andrew and Andre had hauled water and washed clothes by the river. Each day was a continuous cycle of suffering and hunger.

The rainy season brought the danger of mosquitoes that increased the probability of malaria. Rats snuck into the boys' hut at night and scurried around for any sign of crumbs. Cockroaches the size of Texas scampered around their heads in the middle of the night. Andre mentioned that the most bothersome time was at night when red fire ants would cover their bodies as they lay on the damp floor. The dreaded Black Mamba, a large deadly snake, would slither into their village and frighten the orphans.

It is culturally encouraged to beat children at a very young age. Zambians take the verse "Withhold not correction from the child: for if thou beatest him with the rod, he shall not die" (Prov. 23:13) as an excuse to execute corporal punishment. The beatings can even occur well beyond the teen years. Victoria spoke about the punishment. "If an adolescent is too old to be beaten by their parents, then they hire a person to do the beating. The child is brought out to the woods for seven days. They are commanded to take off all their clothes, and then it is the job of the 'beater' to cover the child's body with a clay mud. During the week out in the woods, the 'beater' can do whatever he wants to the child. They receive terrible beatings and pinchings. After a week, all of the people in the village gather around the child, and she/he proceeds to tell her parents what she had learned."

"Did you have to go into the woods with a 'beater'?" I winced as I asked Victoria the question.

Wide-eyed and with a sigh of relief, Victoria said, "No, no, I was afraid of being sent into the woods; therefore, I would obey my grandmother."

On the other hand, the boys were beaten with pipes for being five minutes late to school, for being disrespectful, for stealing a mango off a tree, or for not finishing a daily chore. An endless cycle of silent suffering hovered over the village.

We soon discovered that Victoria was industrious and always woke up at five a.m. She would iron the boys' clothes before the roosters crowed. She later explained that all the clothes had to be ironed because, when they were hung out to dry, maggots would cling to the clothes. Then when a person would put on his clothes the maggots would burrow under their skin and multiply. This description convinced me that every piece of clothing needed to be ironed!

Only 8% of adolescents reach high school. High schools consist of boarding schools in the capital city.

Each day at the guesthouse I took out school supplies and examined the educational level of the children. To our disappointment, the boys, who were not English speaking, did not even recognize the alphabet (even though letters were the same in the Bemba language as in English). The boys were ten years old and had never read a book. They had uniforms but had only sporadically attended school. Even though I taught special education in the US, I quickly realized that I was ill-prepared for the educational challenge I faced with the boys. Victoria willingly translated the Bemba language into English as we tried to communicate with the boys.

On the other hand, Victoria, who was fourteen years old and had been raised in Lusaka, both spoke and read English. However, she lacked the academic English skills needed to be successful in American schools.

The more time we spent with Victoria; the more we began to understand her sweet personality. Victoria has an inner strength that endured daily adversity. Even though she had carried a heavy load since she was a young girl, she still had a lighthearted side to her. She loved Kerry's humor and enjoyed spending time with him. She began to bond with Andrew and Andre and laughed as they explored their new home. Our little family began to develop a routine, enjoy each other, and laugh at silly situations.

The court date was quickly approaching, and I felt confident that the adoption would go smoothly. The night before court, I nervously gathered our paperwork and ironed the children's clothes for the morning. Little did we know that court time would be wrinkled with trouble.

Meeting the boys for the first time

Andrew and Andre walking to Victoria's home on the first day
we met the children.

First time meeting Andrew and Andre's family in their home.
Sharing goodies with the children.

Meeting Victoria and her grandmother for the first time
in the village.

Chapter 4
Court Chaos

The next morning everyone woke up to roosters crowing. We scurried around the guesthouse to get ready for an early court date. The children again sat at the breakfast table at five a.m. waiting for me to prepare the baby porridge I purchased at a local market. Feeding the children baby porridge gave them the extra nutrition they craved and added much needed calories to their diet. They were relieved that there was food to consume and ravenously ate all of the cereal. I could not eat since my stomach was in knots, as I contemplated the importance of the court date. Meanwhile, Kerry continued to sleep.

We had eagerly awaited this day for a year and a half. Since we had been in Zambia for less than forty eight hours, I was unfamiliar with the culture and did not know what to expect. Fear crept into my heart, and my hands began to tremble. To my relief, Kerry reassured me and prayed that the Lord would direct our path and give us the strength for the day.

Teri, our missionary friend, promptly picked us up for court. Paperwork was neatly organized, the children looked their best, and nervous energy was in the air as we boarded the van. The boys were excited to ride in the vehicle even though they did not know where we were going.

Before we left for Zambia, we had been assured by the social worker that the paperwork was in order. When we arrived at the local court in Ndola, we were hopeful that the adoption proceedings would be successful. When we glanced into the small office, we saw how ill-equipped they were. Sitting in the stifling environment were four officials at adjacent desks who shared a single ink pen. It was now obvious that all of Zambia even had a shortage of pens! In the courthouse, there were no supplies such as copy machines, staplers, or paperclips. To have a computer was a distant dream. The stark white building sorely needed a gallon of paint and had bars on the windows. The building lacked basic amenities such as bathrooms, a waiting area to sit down, air conditioning, and a drinking fountain.

We had arranged for a taxi to pick up the children's grandmothers in the village, along with Pastor Bernard, who had assisted with the adoption. Sitting in the hot sun, we patiently waited for the social worker who had all the paperwork. As the court time loomed, we frantically began to call the social worker. Even though we had paid for a taxi to pick him up, precious minutes ticked by waiting for him to arrive. Meanwhile, I paced along the side of the building like a caged lion, hoping to catch a glimpse of his arrival. After an hour, the sun rose higher, and its piercing rays reflected off the stark white building. Anger ascended in me like a smokestack bellowing with black soot.

> The Zambian judicial system is hampered by inefficiency, corruption, and a lack of resources, according to the U.S. Department of State (2012).

Finally, I caught a glimpse of a yellow taxi pulling around the bend. The social worker had arrived an hour late. As we were ushered in by court officials, we were surprised to find out that the judge was also an hour late.

Like frantic mice in a maze, we scurried down a multitude of narrow hallways. At last we stood outside the magistrate's office. I stopped to gather my thoughts, wondering if this was the beginning of a complicated day. We entered a courtroom that was the size of a closet and squeezed in like sardines. The magistrate was a heavy-set man who sat hunched over his desk. A burly man, he sat grunting and scowling as he scribbled on his notepad. It became apparent that the magistrate in charge of the proceedings had a chip on his shoulder. Andrew and Andre sat still on our laps, apparently too afraid to move. Then Kerry, Pastor Bernard and I quietly approached the magistrate's desk. Knowing that women had little value in their culture, I did not look at the judge or dare say a word. Without ever looking at us, he began to flip through the paperwork.

Kerry and I were sending up S.O.S. prayers as the tension rose like mercury in a thermometer. As the proceedings continued, the magistrate moaned and sighed as he shuffled through the paperwork. At last he addressed Kerry with one piercing question.

Barely audible due to his raspy voice, he inquired: "How long have you been in Zambia?"

My hands began to sweat. Silence permeated the walls of the chamber. We knew that if we told him the truth about the length of our actual stay, it would minimize our chances of being able to adopt the boys. A single word could change the fate of the children's lives. Kerry, true to his convictions, immediately decided not to give the coached answer of "four months." Refusing to lie, Kerry answered the question: "Five days."

The judge's eyes were fixed on us, a look of disbelief on his face. In that crystallized moment, we knew we had lost the adoption case. The magistrate then reprimanded the social worker for not having proper paperwork. The social worker responded by stumbling through with excuse after excuse. Everything in me wanted to plead for the lives of the children, but Kerry's hand on my arm communicated that any more dialogue would jeopardize the entire adoption. We were then dismissed. A court date of seven days later was stamped on our paperwork. At that moment, Kerry spoke up and requested an earlier court date, but it was denied and we were ushered out of the chambers.

> More than a quarter million children do not attend school and 47% of those enrolled in school do not complete the primary grades.

I sat outside the chambers hunched over, stunned by what had just transpired. I felt that I was in the middle of a bad dream.

In disbelief, I asked Kerry, "In a matter of minutes! How could things fail so quickly? Will we ever be able to adopt these three children, or are we chasing a wild fantasy?" Three precious lives were at stake, and Kerry and I were determined to fight for them.

After speaking with the court recorder, we discovered that the social worker had not successfully completed the paperwork—even though we had sent him thousands of dollars to make sure it was done properly before we arrived. The money demanded of us was becoming insurmountable. Nothing is without a trail of costs in Zambia. By the time we left the social worker's office, we had again handed over money for papers to be signed. We then took a five-hour road trip to the capital city in a frantic attempt to correct the incomplete paperwork. When we arrived, key officers in Lusaka requested extra funds to complete even the simplest form. It was business as usual in Zambia. Kerry and I continued to struggle with paying bribes, or, as Zambian officials call them, "gifts."

As we encountered the customs of the culture of filtering money, we soon realized that we would be unable to adopt the kids without giving even more money. We hesitantly decided to align ourselves with the demands of the officials by wiring money from the US. We were reminded of these verses: "You, Lord, are my lamp; the Lord turns my darkness into light. With your help, I can advance against a troop; with my God I can scale a wall. As for God, his way is perfect: The Lord's word is flawless; he shields all who take refuge in Him. For who is God besides the Lord? And who is the Rock except our God? It is God who arms me with strength and keeps my way secure. He makes my feet like the feet of a deer; he causes me to stand on the heights" (Ps. 18:29-33).

Even though we were disappointed with the delayed court date, the extra time gave us more insight into the Zambian culture. Gas was ten dollars a gallon, and only the rich are fortunate enough to have a vehicle. The main method of transportation was on foot or local buses. We noticed that Zambians were walking several miles to get to places. We watched a young woman with a baby strapped on her back while carrying a ten-gallon jug of water on her head. Groceries were triple the cost of what they were in the States, and meat was a rare commodity.

Many of the people in the village ate birds, termites, caterpillars, and snakes for protein. But in the midst of their suffering, there was a quiet and calm demeanor about the Zambian people, who were warm and personable. They are the most patient people on the planet, always waiting hours on end for any service. On the other hand, I did not like to wait day after day for another court date. As the week passed, I knew that the only way to survive the constant delays was to seek the Lord for His deliverance.

Desperately trying to maintain a schedule for the kids in our little guesthouse, I began schooling the children a few hours each day. Since the boys were non-English speaking, teaching was a huge challenge. Teaching basic living skills, going to the market each day, and cooking easy-to-digest meals became my priorities. During one of our mealtimes, I asked Victoria to translate and ask the boys if they had received any of the food Kerry and I sent to them. Before we arrived in Zambia, we sent a thousand dollars to be used to sustain the children. We wanted to provide food for the children while we were still in the States.

The boys told Victoria that they had only received a small amount of corn meal, which was worth only a few cents. I was outraged that we had sent money for food and they had never received it. When I asked Victoria the same question, she began to weep, tears rolling down her face. I asked her if she had been hungry, and she said, "Yes, my grandmother and me had been without food."

In between her tears she sobbed, "We were starving!"

At that instant, Kerry had to hold me back from calling the authorities. I sat in disbelief, trying to comprehend the corruption that engulfed this culture. The gravity of the situation felt like a heavy weight on my chest. Money was being pilfered at my children's expense. Brokenhearted, tears now streamed down my face. It was too much for me to bear. Kerry then quietly reminded me to lay the burden down before the Lord. Our Lord is just and cares for the orphans far more than we humanly can, he reminded me.

As Kerry and I read the Bible that night, we came across a verse in Isaiah 43 that comforted our hearts. "When you go through the

41

waters I will be with you; and through the rivers, they will not go over you; when you go through the fire you will not be burned; and the flame will not have a power over you" (43:2).

Soon after, we hired a taxi so we could continue the arduous adoption process. Early in the morning I gazed out the taxi window and saw a young woman with a baby strapped on her back, sitting on top of a large rock pile. She had a rock in her hand and was hitting larger rocks in order to make smaller rocks. The young woman's goal was to sell the gravel that she made. At the end of the day, as we returned to the guesthouse, I glanced out of the taxi window and could not believe my eyes. I saw the same woman on top of the rock pile working as hard as she had eight hours earlier. I felt pity for the woman and realized how much females suffered in Zambia.

Kerry and I found ourselves in a time warp. Just like the movie Groundhog Day, where Bill Murray finds himself stuck living the same day over and over again, we too were reliving each day. After patiently waiting seven days, we had high expectations of appearing in court to finalize the adoptions. It was eventually revealed to us that the social worker was still in the capital city of Lusaka, which was four hours away. We had been led to believe that he had returned the night before the court date. We wondered how many more days we would be allowed to be in Zambia before our paperwork expired. We had to wait and wait as we put our lives in America on hold.

It became increasingly more difficult to wait as the days passed, knowing that we had other children in the States. Anxiety crept into my life like slow-moving volcanic lava. I knew that Kerry's and my leave of absences from our employers were also quickly coming to an end. Waiting became like a vice pressing in on both sides. I was being crushed between two worlds. There was nothing to do but to surrender the burden to the Lord. In despair, I opened the Bible and searched for comfort from God's Word.

"For my thoughts are not your thoughts, neither are your ways my ways, declares the LORD" (Isa. 55:8). I humbly bowed my head and entrusted my troubles to the Lord. With surrender came strength from the Lord.

In order to save our sanity, we continued to maintain a schedule for the kids. Daily schooling was a challenge since the boys lacked the skills needed to memorize the alphabet. I was a special education teacher and knew the educational hurdle that the twins were facing. I constantly tried to evaluate whether their deficit was from a learning disability or malnourishment. My patience began to wane each day as I tried to engrave a few letters in their memory. Songs, rhymes, dances, all failed to seep into their memory. On the other hand, Victoria, despite the many educational gaps, was able to comprehend and memorize facts. Daily she worked on basic math and reading skills to improve her English.

> Over 85% of the nation is considered below the poverty line.

Going to the market daily was an adventure in itself. One US dollar is the equivalent to five thousand Kwatchas (Zambian currency). Holding fifty dollars' worth of Kwatchas in my pocket made me feel like a millionaire. Buying a bottle of Coke cost five thousand Kwatchas, which meant we were carrying a huge pile of cash! We were constantly looking over our shoulders, knowing our Caucasian presence made us an easy target for robbers.

> Almost 1 in every 15 children in developing countries dies from hunger.

Kerry and I learned to enjoy peanut butter sandwiches for lunch and dinner while the children ate meat and high protein cereal along with a large amount of fruit. During dinner Andrew explained that, in the village, if they were fortunate enough to have chicken, their grandmother would wring the neck and pluck the chicken. Afterwards, they would eat the legs, eyes, and every part of the animal. When I served chicken one evening we heard loud crunching sounds. After eating the chicken off the bone, Andrew was eating the chicken leg bone like it was a piece of candy. "This is the best part, sucking the marrow out of the middle of the bone," Andrew stated matter-of-factly in the Bemba language.

He also added that they ate pineapple skins. I asked, "Doesn't that hurt your stomach?"

"No, it tastes good!" Andrew exclaimed.

One extremely hot day, I could not resist taking the children to an ice cream shop. Their eyes lit up with excitement as they tasted ice cream for the first time. It was as good as it looked! Imagine trying to teach children how to lick an ice cream cone; it became inevitable that one large scoop plopped on the floor!

The children began to build a sense of security and trust as their physical and emotional needs were met. One of the emails that I wrote during the many days of waiting read as follows:

November 11, 2011

After schooling in the grueling heat, we decided to take the kids on a cab ride across town to the local shops. We surprised them by going to the only movie theatre in Zambia to see "Spy Kids," which was beyond their wildest dreams. We were the only ones present in the theater since the two dollar entrance fee was more than most Zambians made in one day. It didn't matter what movie they saw: it was spectacular!!!

Previously, the boys had given all their little toys we had brought them to the children in the village. As we passed a shop, I noticed little toy cars. While in Zambia I have not seen one child with a toy; therefore, we did not want to indulge the twins. If a child gets two meals a day, he is considered spoiled. But I gave in and all my parenting self-talk went out the window. After a week of watching the boys play with sticks, we bought them two small cheap plastic cars, and they proceeded to play hours upon hours with them.

When I took Victoria to the market, she didn't beg for sweets or baked goods, but she negotiated with me on how many potatoes to buy or how much meat we should have for supper. The children rarely ate meat in the village, which resulted in a lack of protein and affected their growth. If the children were given a piece of meat during the day, they were considered privileged.

Victoria had interesting questions for Kerry and me, since she had rarely encountered a white couple in Zambia. She asked questions like, "What are those dots on your face (freckles)? Why is your hair so smooth? Why do you have those gold things in the back of your teeth?" Victoria concluded that we were rich by counting our cavity fillings.

After a long humid afternoon, Kerry was waiting outside our guest house to catch a local bus, so he could continue with the paperwork. He sat down to eat a packed sandwich. Then a mother and her baby sat next to him on a bench. After a brief conversation, Kerry learned that the mother and baby had not eaten in days. They were starving. He immediately handed over his sandwich, which the mother and baby gobbled up in a few minutes. Kerry was able to share about the love of Jesus as they ate. He then gave the mother money for their bus. As Kerry watched the pair leave, he realized that the Gospel is much more than words.

In Christ,
Kerry and Nancy Frantz

Victoria transformed into a young lady.

Children curious about the microwave
and watching popcorn pop.

Chapter 5
In You the Orphan Finds Mercy

One hot and muggy day, not only did we lose power but the water was also shut off, which was a common occurrence. When the power goes out in Zambia, it becomes pitch black outside, with no lights to be seen for miles around. Prior to the outage, there was a wedding on the grounds of our guesthouse. I observed that the bride and groom ate first while the guests watched. Then the guests received a small portion of food. The party was held in a makeshift building that was at least 110 degrees inside. Traditional African dances were performed by the wedding party. While the people were crammed into the small building, a blackout occurred.

Even though I was the only one on the grounds that had a candle, the guests tried to continue the festivities in the dark. Andrew, Andre, and Victoria had never witnessed a wedding and were glued to the window of the small shelter. After several hours, the lights came back on, and the kids joyfully danced and sang. Kerry and I laughed because the children never had electricity or running water in the village; we realized their new life would be vastly different from what they were used to.

> It is taboo for a bride to eat eggs because it may affect her fertility. Another Bemba tradition is to serve the newlyweds a pot of chicken whose bones are then replaced in the pot and given to the bride's mother.

Each day I struggled with the delayed court date. Even though I enjoyed spending time with the children and educating them, I became more anxious as time went on. My strong-willed personality drove me to persevere, but I also knew that my boldness could jeopardize the adoption. A woman's role in Zambian society was vastly different from that in American culture, and I realized that I had to be passive. At night, when the children were tucked into bed, I would pace back and forth like a caged lioness trying to protect her cubs. I felt helpless as the officials refused to move forward with the adoption process. Finally, one sunny afternoon we were called by an official to appear at court and complete the paperwork.

As our family traveled by taxi to the lawyer's office, there was a loud sound as a tire blew out. The taxi driver worked hard to control the car as it swerved to the side of the road. He proceeded to open his trunk to get the spare tire; to our dismay, the trunk was empty. We were now stranded on the side of the dirt road.

To add to the already stressful situation, when I glanced at Andre, tears were rolling down his face. I reached over and felt his forehead to discover that he had a high fever. Knowing we had limited time to get to the court office, we contacted our missionary friend, Dan. He came and rescued us from the side of the road. As we traveled, I casually mentioned that Andre had a fever. He abruptly turned the vehicle around and headed to the health clinic. The day had gone from bad to worse, and I was feeling overwhelmed by the situation that confronted us.

Not knowing what to expect at the clinic, I hesitantly entered the door of a small run-down building. We spoke to two nurses sitting at a small desk and requested a malaria test for Andre. The nurses quickly administered the test without asking any questions, and they only requested a small fee to pay upfront. We obviously did not look like Andre's biological parents, but it didn't seem to matter who we were or who was being tested. To our surprise, Andre tested positive for malaria. For the rest of the week Andre fought the sickness and had a high fever. We were thankful that we caught the malaria early because in many cases it can be deadly.

We were exhausted by the time we arrived back at the guesthouse and I tucked the children into bed, but we were grateful that the Lord had surrounded us with His goodness. Late that night I tossed and turned as I tried to sort out the day's events. I wondered how many more difficult days we had ahead of us. I felt that each day was a battle, not only to survive the harsh environment but also to make our way up the mountain we had to climb in order to finalize the adoption.

Later that week, after Andre recuperated, we revisited the lawyer's office, only to be disappointed again with lack of progress toward the adoptions.

However, Pastor Bernard created a good ministry opportunity during our long wait between court dates. He arranged for us to assist him with food distribution for the orphans in the Baluba Village. After loading up the supplies and the children, we traveled along a rough, bumpy road to the village. I was uncertain how Andre, Andrew and Victoria would react when they returned back to the village. I hoped the children would help their friends who were in the same desperate situation they had escaped. As I glanced over at Victoria, I marveled at how quickly she had changed. While living in the village, Victoria worked diligently to help her grandmother and took life seriously. Many nights she would stay up all night, trying to comfort her ailing grandmother. She struggled daily to gather enough food for her grandparents to sustain them.

However, her formerly somber demeanor had been transformed; she was now a sweet young girl who loved to laugh. Victoria enjoyed Kerry's sense of humor, as he constantly kept the boys entertained with his antics.

I was also concerned about how Victoria would feel about going back to her grandmother. As we entered the village, children flocked around our vehicle. We were ushered into a small open air building and met by elderly African women who were counting beans. Each orphan would receive the exact same number of beans. As tedious as it seemed, our family gladly helped with the counting and bagging of the rice and beans. It was obvious that limited funds had been received from donors in the US who sponsored the orphans. If an orphaned child had been sponsored by an American family through IN Network (the same organization that we used to sponsor Victoria), that child would receive his monthly stipend. In March 2011, there were 120 chosen orphans out of 350 children that were part of the monthly distribution.

As we all sat on the cement floor counting the beans to place into the small bags, my heart ached as I realized that the little stipend would have to feed an entire clan of each orphan's extended family for a month. My thoughts flashed back to my home in the US. Like most Americans, I had a fully stocked pantry and an abundance of food in the refrigerator. Their starvation was a stark contrast to the three meals a day my children would receive in America. The harsh reality of their suffering sank deep into my heart, and I sighed with an overwhelming sadness, trying to focus on being faithful to the task.

> Mortality rate of children under five is 182 per 1000 (nearly one in every five compared to less than 10 per 1000 in the US).

As Andre, Andrew and Victoria helped with the distribution, they realized that their living situation had vastly changed in the last seven days. The three kids had smiles on their faces and were fully content from all their needs being met. My children, who had been in the same line one month ago, felt relief that they were no longer the recipients of the distribution. They somberly sat on the ledge of the wall as they watched the children line up for the food. I could scarcely imagine my children in the long line waiting patiently while their stomachs ached for food. The situation made me wonder why God had chosen Andrew, Andre, and Victoria out of the 350 orphans in the village. Even more daunting was God choosing these three children out of the one-and-a-half million orphans in Zambia.

The 120 orphans grew hungry as they waited patiently in line for hours to receive their small bag of rice and beans. Desperate poverty was in the sea of faces. Pastor Bernard then directed the children and several adults to sit down and listen to the hope of the Gospel. As Pastor Bernard interpreted, Kerry graciously shared about the love of Jesus and how He gave his life for sinners like us. When Kerry said, "Jesus is our bread of life," the young children nodded their heads in agreement. Christ's love in the Gospel shone as radiant as the sun. Beneath the suffering was a wonderful message of God's love. During the invitation over a hundred children prayed the salvation prayer and then proceeded to receive their food. Their ages ranged from three to eighteen years old. An expression of desperation was on many of their faces. Several small children of about six and seven years old even held babies on their hips as they tried to gather their food. Kerry and I were also able to pack 150 new soccer shorts to be distributed. Even though there was excitement in the air as we prepared to distribute the shorts, we were soon informed by Pastor Bernard that there were not enough shorts for each orphan.

Before Kerry and I left for Zambia, we failed to take the time to count every pair of shorts that were donated. Consequently, there were not enough shorts for every orphan. Pastor Bernard explained to us that, if each orphan could not each receive a pair of shorts, then we should not distribute them. It would be too discouraging for the children who did not receive them.

I thought of a missionary who had faced insurmountable odds in Haiti. Dr. Frechette wrote

> *Poverty is a terrible and ongoing assault on human dignity. Yet, wherever and whenever the dignity of a human person is assaulted and in peril, the human spirit seeks desperately to preserve what is most precious within it. It is an absolute wonder how people can find light and hope in the despairing darkness. For we believers, this is the unfailing light of grace, ever present and faithful, and fiercely loyal to carrying out God's work: renewing the face of the earth, renewing the embattled human heart...Yet from the depths of this tragedy many people, with the help of God, and people like you and I, fight valiantly and are able to rise.*

Hours passed in the hot Zambian sun until eventually the last orphan's name was called and the small bags of beans were all given away. The orphans that had not yet been sponsored by a US donor stood silently outside the building, hoping that their names would be called. The disappointed orphans not on the list quietly walked away with their heads down. It was a village of starvation and death with evil ferociously devouring its prey. Poverty can devour all the joy and hope in a child. Miraculously, God shone His light amidst the darkness. As the orphans walked down the dusty road I choked back my tears, realizing we were their only hope for food.

"How can this be?" I cried out to the Lord.

I bowed my head, realizing my ignorance contributed to their suffering. For many years, I did nothing to help those who were hungry. The orphans held onto the hope that their names would be called next month. It would be a long wait before more food would arrive into the desolate village. The selected orphans knew that their food came down from heaven to them, the weak and vulnerable.

The next day we woke up and scrambled to get ready for the long awaited court date. I had barely recovered from the impact of the previous day. Upon arriving, we again discovered that the social worker was not on time. It was like a reoccurring bad dream. As I paced back and forth outside the courtroom, I peered around the corner of the dilapidated building and prayed that he would arrive. I had never felt angrier or more frustrated. I had concluded that this was the last chance we had for the adoption.

We called for a taxi for the two grandmothers so they could join us at court just in case they had to testify. At last the social worker finally arrived, informing us he did not have enough copies of the documents because his printer had run out of ink. Shocked over the situation, my anger began to boil over like hot water in a kettle. Thankfully, Kerry jumped into action. He and the social worker frantically ran across town to copy the documents onto a thumb drive. They had to have a copy of the documents in hand for court. After ten long minutes with sweat on their brows, they sprinted back with papers in hand.

As we entered the courthouse, we discovered we had missed our court time. As we peered into the judge's humble chambers, it appeared as if smoke was rising out of his nostrils, reminding me of a bull locked in a stall. He had no patience for the ineptness of the social worker and slapped us with a ruling of contempt of court. I stood in the doorway shocked as desperation swept over me. How could I explain to the children that their own country had failed them? I grabbed the doorposts, trying to brace myself with the fact that we had little hope of ever adopting Andrew, Andre, and Victoria.

We were then advised by an official to wait by the courthouse for the rest of the day, "just in case there was an opening in the docket."

Waiting hour after hour in the intense sun, we realized we were in a difficult predicament with two ailing grandmothers who had been dropped off five hours earlier. Andre was still not feeling well and was without anything to drink, causing me to worry that he would become dehydrated.

As we stood there discussing the case, we realized that the sun's rays were beating down with unusual intensity. The missionary informed us of an unusual phenomenon called a "sun burst." She explained that the sun's rays were dangerously hot during the "sun bursts." There was no refuge from the sun surrounding the courthouse, so we began to look for shelter.

We found a local eatery and tried to refresh the grandmothers with locally cooked vegetables. Fatigued by the disappointment of the day, I looked up as court officials approached us. At first I thought we had a court appointment, but my hopes were soon dashed. The officials began to ask for "gifts" to speed up the process. I concluded that those who serve the darkness are consumed by it. After consulting with Pastor Bernard, it became apparent that the bribes would be our last ditch effort to rescue the children from their plight. Even though the judge was nowhere to be found, many envelopes were given to the officials. We walked away from the courthouse without ever going into the building again. I felt deceived and defeated.

Discouragement surrounded me like a hovering dark cloud. I put my arms around the boys and hugged them. Even though we were unable to verbally communicate with each other, the twins sensed my love and smiled up at me. Their look of innocence and vulnerability overwhelmed me. I wanted to snatch them up and carry them home to America. In that split moment, I loved them as my own children and refused to let go. It was too much to bear.

Then a small still voice spoke into my heart. "Nancy, you see, I have given you a portion of My love that I have for the fatherless.

That is why you love them without measure, and that is why you are suffering."

Humbled, I bowed my head and accepted my brokenness, knowing that I was sharing in the suffering of Christ. The sun began to set, and the relief from the penetrating heat was a soothing balm to my soul. We realized we were now twenty miles from our guesthouse, and our only alternative was to take the local bus home. As we walked to the bus, men begged us to buy their small trinkets and became increasingly more aggressive, like bees swarming around honey. The light blue bus was our only ticket out of the potentially dangerous situation.

When it finally arrived, we loaded our three children into the back of the bus; since there was little seating, we let the boys sit on our laps. We noticed some women approaching the bus with baskets containing live chickens on their heads. They were allowed to tie the baskets to the roof of the bus. Chickens squawked and fluttered their wings as the ropes entrapped them in the baskets. Just when the bus was so full that no one could breathe, a center row of seats was folded down the middle to make room for more passengers. To add to the bedlam, the bus driver yelled at a few of the passengers for not paying their fees of thirty cents for each ticket.

> Average gas price was ten dollars a gallon. The high price of gas forced drivers to fill every seat.

Due to the uncomfortable atmosphere, arguments ignited and tempers flared.

My breathing became more difficult, since I had one of the twins on my lap. Windows were opened, but there was not the slightest breeze coming into the bus, making it stifling and unbearable. At last the final seat was filled and the bus departed. All the passengers were squished together like sardines. While chickens squawked from the roof, mothers openly nursed their babies. To add to the misery, the bus stopped every two blocks to let one passenger off and two passengers on.

After riding the bus for an hour, the circumstances became intolerable, and we decided to call Dan to come for us. We were thankful that he came promptly. He wanted to spare us from this difficult cultural experience. By the time we arrived home, the children were exhausted and quiet from the ordeal. They plopped into bed as Kerry and I tried to sort out the chaos of the day. I realized that the adoption process was out of my hands and control. Heartbroken, I bowed my head and pleaded with God to deliver them into our care. I dearly loved Andrew, Andre, and Victoria as much as I did my own biological children. They were orphans that needed our love and parental nurturing.

My prayers seemed to bounce off the ceiling, unanswered and empty. Heaven was silent. Where was my faith? I refused to blame or doubt God, even though I could hardly deal with the gravity of the day. Scriptural verses I had memorized long ago began to wash over my heart. I knew that His promises were true regardless of how I felt. The verse that I rehearsed over and over in my mind was "I will never leave you nor forsake you" (Deut. 31:6). This verse comforted me like a cool breeze in the middle of the desert. I desperately cried out to the Lord to rescue the children. Then I remembered a verse from I Peter 4: "But rejoice insofar as you share Christ's sufferings, that you may also rejoice and be glad when his glory is revealed" (4:13). I was reassured by His Word and knew that the Lord was walking by my side. There was a purpose for my pain.

The next day was Sunday, and worship was our primary focus. Kerry gently reminded me that we needed to give praise where praise was due. As we entered the church, a soft breeze blew through the open windows. Rows of chairs filled up every available space. We ended up sitting in opposite rows, shoulder to shoulder with other believers. The boys sat quietly, feet swaying under their chairs. As the pastor spoke, my soul searched for the promises I had once memorized. As His Word washed over me, I laid at His throne the corruption we encountered in Zambia, along with the bribes, the mistreatment of orphans, and mostly the uncertainty of the adoption of our three children.

Following the distribution, Andrew, Andre, Victoria, and Nancy
visit the orphans in Balboa Village.

Kerry used Gospel picture books to share
Christ with the orphans.

Chapter 6
Oceans Apart

Our third court date finally arrived, and again we were ready at the crack of dawn. When we appeared before the magistrate, he refused to agree to the adoption because, once again, the paperwork was not completed correctly. It became apparent that our stay was rapidly coming to an end; therefore, the next day Kerry made one last effort and traveled to the court. He waited outside for the entire day, trying to get an appointment with the judge, but the magistrate never showed up to work. The entire day was lost.

As I waited for Kerry's arrival, I paced back and forth from the house to the gate. I began to weigh our options. I contemplated different housing situations for the children if the adoption failed. Returning Victoria back to the village was out of the question. I recalled that her grandmother had asked me several times if Victoria had "become a woman yet." Even though Victoria was thirteen years old, she had not had her menstrual cycle, partly due to her low body fat and malnutrition. Later that week I discovered that young girls who "become a woman" are subjected to a two-day tribal ritual. Girls paint their faces and perform tribal dances as the entire village celebrates their womanhood. Consequently, these young girls are preyed upon by older men. Polygamy is a common practice in Zambia, and Victoria would be vulnerable to such treatment. I wanted her to be protected from harm. Her innocence was a treasure, not to be tampered with.

At last Kerry pushed open the gate, and I saw the long expression on his face. I immediately knew the outcome.

Kerry flatly said, "It's over. The judge never showed up to court today. We have lost the case."

My mouth dropped in disbelief.

"No, it cannot be," I quietly said. Kerry and I both realized we had lost the battle and would have to leave the children behind.

My inner turmoil only heightened my despair. My strong-willed personality, which had driven me to persevere during the adoption, was now quenched. I had to relinquish the fight. I had always known God was present in my life and was always working out His purpose; but that day I searched for answers, and I had to desperately rely on His strength. I wanted to hide under His wings to find solace and refuge.

As I walked into the guesthouse I looked at the children reading the book *Brown Bear, Brown Bear, What Do You See?*.

Victoria was rolling on the floor, bellowing out a hearty laugh as the boys tried to pronounce each word. I sat on the edge of the chair, marveling at God's protection of Andrew, Andre, and Victoria. God's presence was in our midst. Jesus would not leave or abandon us, and His love permeated our hearts.

Kerry and I then retreated to the bedroom, sadly realizing that we would have to break the news to the children. Since Victoria was the eldest, we decided to tell her first. Sweet Victoria was the apple of my eye, and I knew that God had her in the palm of His hand. We took Victoria into our bedroom and sat her down. She sat poised on the end of the bed, uncertain of what was happening.

"Victoria," I said in a hushed voice as I held her hand, "We love you and wanted you to be part of our family in America. But the judge has decided not to allow the adoption."

Disbelief and shock were written on her face at that moment, and she crumbled on the bed, sobbing. "Where will I go? Who will I live with?" she asked, as she gasped for breath.

"I don't know yet, but it would be best for you not to return to the village," I said as tears streamed down my face.

"What about the boys?" Victoria asked, since she had already bonded with the boys.

"Andrew and Andre will not be returning with us to America either," I quietly answered.

As we sat on the edge of the bed, Kerry began to share that God is still a loving and faithful God, and He will not abandon us.

Next we explained the news to the boys. As we approached them, I questioned if they would be able to understand that they too would not be coming home with us to America. With so many existing orphans in the village, I wondered who would take care of them. We sat the boys down on the couch, and, with Victoria translating, the boys took in the gravity of the situation. Andrew had his hands folded on his lap as tears welled up in his eyes. The disappointment was too great for him. Andre sat quietly, trying to absorb the situation. The sad expression on his face told me that he finally understood what we were saying to them. Then he laid his head down and cried.

Our small family sat in silence, trying to sort through our despairing feelings. All of this heartache was too much for a mother to take. Feelings of helplessness swept over me. I wrapped my arms around the gaunt shoulders of Andre and Andrew as I struggled to remain strong. I could not let go of the children. Like a rushing waterfall my tears descended down my cheeks. A dark cloud hovered over our guesthouse, and sorrow engulfed us. I prayed for strength and comfort. Even though Andrew, Andre, and Victoria would be continents away, I understood that our hearts would be closely knitted together.

We were then confronted with the challenge of finding a home for the children. Kerry and I had forty-eight hours before we flew back to the US. We realized that the boys would be the most difficult to place because of their young ages and their inability to speak English. In Zambian culture the young boys had no value as workers, whereas Victoria, who was older and more industrious, could contribute to a household.

We decided to use the rest of our finances to find a home for them. I was aware that, with over one-and-a-half million orphans in Zambia, finding a home for Andrew, Andre, and Victoria would be nearly impossible. Rain was descending in torrents, along with my tears. We were facing an insurmountable task. Returning to the village again was not an option. Without any supervision or food to sustain them, the boys would become vulnerable. After calling several missionaries, an orphanage in the capital city became a viable option; however, by the end of the day we found out that the orphanage was full. We were quickly running out of choices. My strong will drove me to frantically continue looking for a home for the children.

"Lord," I prayed, "You are the Father to the fatherless; I beg You to provide a home for the boys."

After long deliberations with Pastor Bernard and Medica, they committed to take care of Andrew and Andre until we returned to Zambia. They already had five children; therefore, it would be a great sacrifice to take care of two more. Washing clothes in an outside basin (with electricity turned off more than it was on) and going to the market daily makes life difficult for a mother. I realized having seven children in one small home would add extra work and stress to an already difficult situation. But I was grateful and relieved that God had provided a safe refuge for Andrew and Andre.

Kerry and I now had to secure a home for Victoria. I made several calls to missionaries, but they were all unable to take care of her. The missionaries recommended that we put Victoria in an orphanage in Lusaka. We became increasingly uncomfortable with the recommendation, speculating that she would be too vulnerable with other boys in the compound. I obtained several contact numbers that could be a possible placement for Victoria, and I began to call complete strangers, begging them to help us. Not knowing the environment that Victoria would live in made me nervous for her safety. When the sun began to set, I had still not secured a home for her. I became frantic about her well-being.

Becoming frustrated with the dead-end phone calls, I decided to pack. As I was scurrying around the guesthouse, sorting our belongings and putting the kids to bed, there was a light knock on the door. Dan, the missionary from whom we were renting, sat down in our humble guesthouse. He typically jokes around and is lighthearted, but tonight, with sweat dripping from his brow, he was worn out and serious. He had a message to relay to us. In the dimly lit room, Dan settled back in the couch with a shadow cast on his face. Even though he was in his early thirties, I noticed deep lines around his eyes and the weariness etched in his brow. The corruption and desperation of the culture had taken its toll on him.

Dan looked directly at us and, with a somber expression, asked a piercing question. "Are you intending to come back for Victoria? If you are not coming back for her, then it is in her best interest to return to the village immediately."

Unaware of the village ritual, Dan felt it would be better for her not to continue in a life of security and comfort, if she would eventually end up back in the village as a result of a failed adoption.

But Kerry emphatically said, "We will never give up on Victoria, and we will work hard while we are in the States to move the adoption forward." Upon hearing this, Dan somberly said that he and his wife discussed the matter and had decided to take Victoria into their home.

With a forlorn look in his eyes, Dan deeply sighed. I knew he was sacrificing his last amount of his energy by committing to take care of Victoria. I wanted to jump up for joy! I tried to constrain my response. I knew that his family was under pressure as they were raising three young children in an unsafe environment. We were elated by the news and thanked the Lord that He had provided for Victoria. When I broke the news to Victoria, a penetrating smile lit up her face. "Mom, I am happy that I am going to live with them," Victoria triumphantly told me.

Late that night I finished packing separate bags for the children. My heart was shattered as I weighed the gravity of the situation. Questions lurked in my mind. Would we ever be successful in adopting the children? How long will it be before we are able to return with the correct paperwork in place?

The boys were confused about where they were going to live. Andrew and Andre did not believe we would ever come back for them. When Kerry and I told them that America was across the world, Andrew and Andre had difficulty believing that they would ever become part of our family. The twins had already experienced many disappointments and heartaches in their lives, and now they had to face another major crisis. In order to provide for the twins, I packed envelopes with cash so they would be able to go to school.

The next morning our little family traveled with us to Lusaka for the next day's flight. The last day we were together we had a wonderful night in a guesthouse. It was a pleasant night as we sat on the quaint porch eating pizza. It was the first time they had eaten pizza, and they enjoyed every bite! I did not mind that the electricity was off, as we sat under the reflection of the moonlight. The night was calm, the surrounding flowers gave off a rich aroma, and, most importantly, we were laughing and singing, savoring our last moments together. Later that night, Kerry read the Bible to the children, and we prayed for God's grace. As we tucked the boys into bed, we all realized this would be the last time Kerry and I would be able to give them a goodnight kiss. If only time could stand still. If only I could sweep the kids away to America. God's plan was a mystery to me. But that night I surrendered the children into His hands, and peace swept over me like a warm blanket.

The next morning, we loaded the car to go to the airport and arranged for a driver to take the children back to Ndola, where their new homes would be. As we traveled to the airport, Andrew's and Andre's faces were pensive, their life of suffering etched on their young faces. Victoria's deep brown eyes were no longer twinkling in the light as she gazed out of the car window. As soon as we entered the airport, the attendant announced our flight. Dread swept over me, and I could not get myself to walk toward the terminal. Our family gathered around and huddled in a circle trying to say goodbye. The reality of leaving the children was more than I could bear. A feeling of grief engulfed me like a thick black cloud as tears streamed down my face.

I hugged Victoria's thin frame, longing to be her mother and provide for her needs. The three children had already lost their biological parents; how could they lose us, too? Andrew, Andre, and Victoria still remained orphans, vulnerable and exposed to the harsh realities of not having parents to care for them.

I gathered the boys in my arms and hugged them. With their thin arms draped around my neck, I wondered if I would ever see them again. I loved them as my own children. As a little family, we knelt in the middle of the airport and prayed for our gracious Lord to have mercy on us. Then Kerry gently nudged my elbow, and I knew it was time to board the plane. I took comfort in the knowledge that we had entrusted the children into the Lord's care. As Kerry and I slowly ascended up the stairs to the plane, I desperately tried to get one more glimpse of the children. I turned one last time and locked eyes with Andrew, Andre and Victoria. My mother's heart was torn into a million pieces. I could hardly catch my breath as we entered the gate area and waved goodbye to them for the last time. I had to let go and give their lives to God, the Father of the fatherless. Again, I was reminded that God's love for Andrew, Andre, and Victoria was greater than any love I could offer them. At last, we boarded the plane to America, leaving the children behind.

Chapter 7
Life in the Fast Lane

In March 2011, Kerry and I returned to America and resumed our daily routine. I was torn between two families, one in America and one in Zambia. In the US, my children needed the stability of a family, and yet my heart longed for the three children in Zambia. Eventually life settled in, and I continued working as a teacher for the visually impaired and blind students. Kerry returned to church to continue his role as an assistant pastor at Grace Presbyterian Church. The congregation rallied behind us and became a continual source of encouragement. Every day we worked on the adoption paperwork, realizing that time was quickly passing. December 31 was the deadline for the approval of the adoptions, and it was only nine months away. We searched for a Zambian lawyer to correctly finish the paperwork.

Meanwhile, we discovered that Dan had become critically ill with malaria. Unfortunately, his wife was in South Africa receiving treatment herself. Victoria took over the household and cared for the young children. Even though Dan received treatment for the malaria, he did not respond to the medicine. He was a young father who faced a serious illness, and he drifted in and out of consciousness. Thankfully, after many days in the local hospital his health began to improve. After hearing the good news of his recovery, we were happy that Victoria had been able to step in to help.

Later that month, Kerry and I were informed that Dan and his wife would be leaving the mission field and returning to the States within a month. A sense of panic again hovered over me like a dark cloud. How was I ever to find a home for Victoria when we lived on different continents? After the shock settled in, I went into high gear in order to find another home for Victoria. After making numerous phone calls to Zambia, I quickly realized I was running out of options. Consequently, I contacted the director of IN Network. The director and his wife decided to provide housing for Victoria. We were relieved that she did not have to be placed in an orphanage, which could potentially put her in danger. Victoria was placed in her new home and started private school; however, like an approaching storm, poor Victoria had to face another adjustment to a new home, guardians, and school. We kept in touch via Skype and noticed her sweet smile began to diminish; her countenance became solemn as she began to doubt whether we would ever come back for her.

Second Trip: A Second Chance

Each day I sought the Lord's guidance and protection for my children both here and on the other side of the world. Early in the morning on October 12, 2011, I checked my email, and, to my relief, we had received a notice from the Zambian lawyer. The new court date was set for just a little over a week away, on October 20th! Kerry and I were notified that we would only be able to adopt the boys at this time and would have to return a third time for Victoria. Even though the news about Victoria was disappointing, we were thankful for the court date and the possibility of adopting Andre and Andrew. Each day I grew more anxious about being with the children and the possibility of watching over their well-being. Kerry and I hurriedly made preparations for our second trip to Zambia. We knew from experience that we faced another daunting trip riddled with corruption and crime.

Unlike our first trip, we would not have the support of Dan and his wife, but, on a positive note, we were familiar with the essential items that were needed for the orphans in the village. Thankfully we were able to bring clothes, school supplies, and theological books for the pastors. Even though saying good-bye to my children in America was difficult, I knew that Andre, Andrew, and Victoria needed a family. After the long twenty-five-hour flight, we eventually landed in Ndola. The sights and sounds were now familiar to me: women carrying baskets on their heads, roosters on the roadside, and the luscious banana trees sprawling across the grasslands.

As I exited the runway, I eagerly searched for Victoria, Andrew, and Andre so I could gather them in my arms. Turning towards the setting sun, I noticed a silhouette of three small figures standing up against the fence with their faces pressed up against the bars, grinning from ear to ear and eager to greet us. Soon the gap of eight months was bridged by one long embrace. It was simply amazing. Victoria looked like a young lady. She had her hair braided and wore a flowing colorful skirt. Her dimples made her smile appear even more innocent. It was evident that God's grace was upon this young lady. Seeing her smile, charm, and warm welcome made the long wait worthwhile. The boys had their hair cleanly cut, and naïve smiles lit up their faces. I noticed they were wearing the clothes that we had left them. It was a sweet reunion. I hugged the boys, who appeared to be the same size they were eight months ago. Victoria and I locked eyes, and, with the long separation now behind us, we hugged each other, never wanting to let go.

As we traveled to our new guesthouse, we chatted about school, how we missed each other, and the possibility of forming a new family. Without the presence of the missionaries, Kerry and I realized we would be even more vulnerable to the corrupt culture. When we approached the new guesthouse, we noticed it was well guarded with barbed wire walls and armed guards. After we entered our humble abode, I distributed a small amount of used toys, clothes, and books. Excitedly, the children gathered around for their newfound treasures, content to be a family again.

As we settled into a routine, the children's ferocious appetites reminded me of hungry lions. I enjoyed cooking for them and was elated that we were once again united. As nightfall was approaching, I ran the bath water for the boys. As I filled the bathtub, I kissed the top of their shaved little heads and discovered squirming varmints on their scalp! Worms again, yuck! I now realized there was a reason why the boys appeared not to have gained any weight. I quickly tried to rinse my mouth in the faucet and then realized the water was unfiltered. The situation had gone from bad to worse. The first priority in the morning was to purchase deworming pills for the boys and myself.

Early the next morning I walked into the kitchen and noticed hamburgers frying on the stove. I had forgotten Victoria's industrious nature. She was cooking lunch at five a.m. Later, as the afternoon approached, I was once again sobered by the reality of raising curious eleven-year-olds. Andrew and Andre managed to light a candle in their room to celebrate their rare find of matches. I knew it would be some time before their first sleepover!

The following Monday morning was a top priority to prepare for the court appointment. We arrived at the lawyer's office; when Andrew greeted the lawyer, he bowed on one knee and then extended his hand to shake hands. I was relieved that Bernard had taught Andrew basic cultural manners. The lawyer informed Kerry and me that we were not to talk to the judge. Instead, we needed to drop our eyes when the judge addressed us, and our answers should be brief. Since the adoption case had been appealed to a higher court, we were thankful to hear that we would be appearing before a different judge.

That night, as Kerry and I sat on the edge of the bed, we prayed and asked the Lord to impart His favor on us. We were reminded of the verse "Religion that is pure and undefiled before God, the Father, is this: to visit orphans and widows in their affliction and to keep oneself unstained from the world" (James 1:27). I was fearful of the court's outcome and had to believe that the Father of the fatherless would be merciful to our family.

On October 20, we nervously arrived at the courthouse. Surprisingly, the social worker was on his best behavior. He was on time and had the correct paperwork in hand.

The air in the courtroom was stifling. The judge sat at the end of a long narrow table, hunched over the paperwork. I felt a sense of intimidation as I sat across from him on a couch. Anxiously, I twirled the edge of my skirt, not daring to move an inch. I prayed a quick prayer that the Lord would be the One to determine the fate of Andrew and Andre. Even though the judge was small in stature, his stern facial expression reminded me of a tied-up bulldog ready to break loose. We all sensed the judge's foul mood. Andrew, Andre, Kerry, and I sat somberly, waiting to be addressed. The atmosphere was tense, and no one dared to speak or glance up at the judge. Finally, he looked up from the paperwork and addressed his concerns about the adoption.

In a deep, low tone, the judge asked Kerry, "Is your salary adequate to provide for five children?"

Ironically, even though our salary was nothing to boast about, it was far beyond that of many wealthy Zambian citizens. Not making eye contact, Kerry responded to the judge's question. After long periods of silence the judge shuffled his papers and then let out a bellowing loud sigh that echoed throughout the chambers. My nervousness escalated like an elevator reaching the top floor.

Without even looking up, the judge stated matter-of-factly, "Adoption approved."

My eyes lit up, and, without making a sound, I smiled at Kerry as he squeezed my hand. We were ushered out of the courtroom, and for the first time Kerry and I embraced Andrew and Andre Mumba Frantz. Unsure if the boys understood why we were elated, Pastor Bernard promptly translated that the adoption was approved. A big smile shone on their faces as we left the room with tears streaming down our faces, rejoicing that the Lord had delivered the children into our hands. Pastor Bernard and Medica rejoiced with us and were undoubtedly relieved that the boys were no longer under their care. As I looked over at Victoria, even though she was smiling slightly, there was a glimmer of disappointment in her eyes as she realized she would be left behind again.

Soon our happiness was tarnished as more "gifts" were requested by the lawyer and social worker for the completion of the adoption.

Even though we realized that we needed to move quickly to Lusaka to obtain the visas, we first wanted to minister to the orphans in the village. Their needs were overwhelming; therefore, I tried to narrow down what were the most pressing needs of the children. When I spoke with Pastor Bernard, I asked him how many children had worms. He said, with a forlorn look, "All of them have worms." Since our boys had a bad case of worms, Kerry and I understood the gravity of the situation. Worms can have devastating effects on the host. In severe cases, the worms can eventually eat through the infested person's stomach lining. It can be painful to have worms, not to mention that they consume any food digested in the stomach, thus preventing the host from receiving any nutritional value. Thankfully, with the donated funds I was able to purchase three-hundred packages of deworming pills. Each treatment cost only a meager forty-nine cents each! I couldn't believe that the needless suffering of the orphans could be easily prevented for just the price of a few meals at a typical fast-food restaurant in America. In addition, we had enough funds for bags of rice and beans.

> 20% of children are AIDS/HIV orphans, an estimated 630,000 in total.

We made the long trip into the village with Andrew, Andre, and Victoria. It was the rainy season in Zambia, and the wet clay roads formed huge ruts. Huts were scattered along the road with young toddlers standing on the side of the road. The deep potholes sent us bobbing up and down like a hook and sinker. As we pulled up in the taxi, the sight and smells overwhelmed me. Steam rose from the tires as we came to a slow stop. Immediately, children came running from all directions and scurried around the car. They busily chattered in the Bemba language, excitedly jumping up and down. The children peered into the car, curious about who the white people were that entered the village.

Shockingly, mothers began to approach the car window and asked me to take their babies to America. It was evidence of the deep love that a mother has for her child to deliver him from this plight.

The sight of the children overwhelmed me. I could hardly catch my breath as I gazed into the hollow eyes of the starving children. Their eyes were glazed over from lack of nutrition. Grimacing faces, legs resembling twigs, and protruding ribs were common features. My heart ached for the hopelessness of these orphans. Their little lives were consumed by poverty, and desperation was written on their faces. It was all I could do to choke back the tears. The children's faces were etched with the fear of suffering from starvation.

Thoughts of my own comfortable home with air conditioning, soft beds, and cupboards full of food, faucets and lights made me wince at the contrast between the two countries. This was not a random TV commercial; these were real children who were suffering and reaching out for help. I held their small frail hands, wanting to protect them from their pain.

Questions swirled in my mind. "Lord, how can these children endure such suffering?"

I lifted my eyes to the heavens and sent out a silent cry to the Lord. "I beg you to save these children from starvation. Lord, how could I be so wasteful, thankless, and blind?"

I stepped back from all the commotion and tried to gather my thoughts. Soft words spoke into my heart.

The still voice whispered, "I love these children, and they are mine. Do you not know that I have saved you, too, from your desperation and sins?" I then understood that the orphans were held in the palm of their Father's hand.

Later, Andre, Andrew, and Victoria gladly helped with the counting of beans for the distribution. Our children were again reminded of village life, grass huts, and no electricity or running water. It was hard to believe that Andre, Andrew, and Victoria were in the line waiting for the food distribution ten months ago. God's mercy had saved them out of extreme poverty.

Several hundred people sat down, waiting for Kerry to bless them with a message from the Bible. Pastor Bernard had gathered the people for Kerry to share the love of Jesus with them. We handed out children's tracts so the people in the village, who were non-English speaking, could follow along by looking at the pictures. After Kerry explained that a person can only have eternal life through faith in Jesus Christ, he then shared a simple prayer to receive Jesus as their personal Savior. The crowd listened intently to the message of hope. Even though they had already waited five hours in the hot sun, they hung on every spoken word. As Pastor Bernard translated, the people prayed the sinner's prayer in the Bemba language. A hush came over the crowd. Hearing them pray with sincerity and out of desperation for their situation was an incredibly moving moment. Heaven came down and settled on the people, giving them strength and faith to continue another day.

The orphans then began to line up outside the small distribution building while the hot sun beat down on them. One by one the orphans were called. As the children received malaria pills, the Zambian women explained to them how to take the medicine. Children as young as three years old were receiving the medicine without adult supervision. As I handed out the medicine to the young children, I prayed a short prayer that no one would steal the medicine from them and that an adult would help them. As the children received their treasured gifts, they curtsied or bowed, then quietly left the building. At the end of the distribution, each child was thankful to have received the stipend of rice, beans, and medicine.

While Kerry stayed back and played with the children, Victoria and I walked toward her grandmother's hut. Even though Kerry didn't have any balls or toys, he was able to show off his talent by teaching them how to juggle ears of corn and use corn stalks as baseball bats with a guava as a ball. For the first time in the village, American baseball was introduced to the children! He also demonstrated his rare ability to touch his tongue to his nose and wiggle his ears without touching them. The children roared with laughter and could not believe such talent.

Meanwhile, Victoria and I traveled down the dusty path to visit with her grandmother and grandfather. We walked down the winding path that was surrounded by grass huts. Naked children played in the dirt as older children stared at the white woman traveling with an African teenager. We were quite the odd sight.

Without any shade to provide relief from the hot sun, I began to wonder how much longer our little family could endure without any water. After ascending a large hill, we finally arrived at her grandmother's home. Victoria's grandmother had an infectious smile as she came running out of her hut to greet us. After a long embrace, we went inside to visit. Her thatched roof was being repaired so dust had settled all over the small home. I explained to her that we would have to travel back to Zambia a third time in order to adopt Victoria. Even though she was discouraged by the news, she was grateful for the care we gave Victoria.

As we left the hut, kids began to flock around Victoria and me. Victoria was like a proud peacock, showing her friends the new math textbook I brought her. As we were walking back, I noticed a set of twin sisters who were each wearing only one shoe. They were sharing a pathetic pair of sandals that were too small for them. Their feet were shuffling in the dirt so they could keep that flimsy broken sandal on one of their feet. As we headed to the car, I had

Andrew and Andre take off their sandals and give them to the girls. The girls were ecstatic that they both had shoes on their feet, and surprisingly, they fit perfectly. The girls grinned from ear to ear. After examining their new shoes, they both ran off, skipping with glee.

The only food I brought for the day was a few apples and peanut butter sandwiches in my backpack. Realizing that the orphaned children who followed Victoria and me were still hungry, I divided up the sandwiches into bite-sized pieces to give to the orphans. As I held up the pieces of apple in the air, several dozen children tried to reach for them. I sighed deeply at the sight of their frail arms reaching desperately for a mere bite of an apple. How could I possibly meet the physical needs of all the hungry children? I emptied every bit of food out of my bag, wishing I had brought more to share. As dusk was quickly approaching, the children happily scurried to their huts. At the end of the exhausting day, we loaded our small family into the taxi. My children were somber from the experience, realizing they could have been the ones reaching for the apple.

Chapter 8
Visiting the dead!

On the home front, our older biological children and Brittany, our adopted daughter, followed our every step. Massive emails were sent to our children for prayer support as we battled for the adoption. Our children were also going through a transition as they tried to imagine life with new siblings. I realized that changing birth order can be traumatic on family members. My last biological child, Bethany, was the youngest until we adopted Brittany. When that happened, Bethany became a middle child. With the adoption prospect of the Zambian children, she would move up the ranks to become the eldest. With all the changes to our family dynamics, older children became a source of prayer support and encouragement to Kerry and me.

Kerry and I realized that moving to the capital city was imperative in order to complete the paperwork. As we traveled five hours by bus to the capital city, it suddenly dawned on me that the boys rarely had traveled outside of their village. The new experience of riding a long distance in a vehicle and the constant motion caused the boys to become ill. Victoria and I sat next to what appeared to be brothers, about seven and ten years old. After several hours, it dawned on me that they did not have any food. After sharing our food, the boys were unable to pay the thirty cents to use the bathroom at the rest stop. When we arrived close to our destination, surprisingly the older boy exited at the bus stop. I could not believe that a young boy was left alone on the bus late at night. After finding out that they were not actually brothers, I was concerned for his safety.

Understanding that we were now in a dangerous situation and at high risk by pulling up to the bus stop past midnight, I firmly instructed the boy to stay with me and hold onto my skirt. As we stepped off the bus, local taxi drivers swarmed around us and pressed against us, demanding our business. The stifling heat and the smell of the bus exhaust were suffocating. I grabbed the shirts of our children as Kerry tried to maneuver through the crowd. Thankfully I spotted Kerry's hand over the rest of the locals. It was troubling to see homeless children begging for food, blind adults reaching out for coins, and prostitutes prowling around the terminal.

We were in the middle of a modern day Sodom and Gomorrah. The licentious atmosphere provoked thoughts of the Biblical account of Lot and his wife fleeing a wicked land.

Trying to shake the thought, I looked down as I exited the bus but then shockingly I realized that the boy from the bus was no longer holding onto my skirt. I frantically searched for him. I yelled into Kerry's ear that the boy from the bus was lost. I then caught a glimpse of a dim silhouette of the boy running in another direction deep into the darkness.

Kerry and the cab driver proceeded to sprint after him, knowing that the boy was in impending danger. I could barely see the men, the fumes from the bus rose above their heads as they dodged around the people. I gathered the children in my arms and moved them into a dark corner to hide from any looming danger. After what seemed to be eternity, I peered around the corner and through the darkness; I saw all three of them walking toward me.

As they strutted toward me, with hands on my hip, I firmly asked why the boy ran away. The boy started to sob, and that he was looking for his aunt that lived in some obscure village. The cab driver then informed me that if they did not get the boy off the other bus, he would have been captured and sold into sex slavery. We loaded into the taxi, dazed from the events of the night. We gave the cab driver money to find the aunt in his village and safely return him. Thankfully, God delivered him from harm and us from the mayhem.

I was again reminded of the dangerous culture that surrounded us when we drove into a facility with armed guards. The humble two-room guesthouse was adequate for our needs. Having running water, electricity, and a refrigerator was a luxury. The air was stifling and oppressive since it was summertime in Zambia. The temperatures rose daily with a heat index of over 105 degrees in November, and the humidity curled my straight hair. Air conditioning was nowhere to be found, and enduring the heat was a way of life. However, the only people who seemed to have difficulty tolerating the heat were Kerry and me. Not having any modern conveniences caused me to search for easier alternatives. I decided not to take the pioneer route of washing our clothes along the river and then drying them on rocks. It was not my idea of fun, and I did not want to have heatstroke, even though the word "wimp" came to mind. Instead I decided to pay a dear maid four dollars a day to launder, hang out, fold, and iron our clothes.

Every day we walked to the market to buy fresh-baked bread and vegetables. We discovered a few facts about Zambia during our second visit:

1. Fans and air conditioning will be featured as a new invention beginning in 2020.

2. Worms do not like de-worming medicine. When it is taken, hundreds of worms will slither through the scalp.

3. Zambians don't believe in modern appliances such as dishwashers, microwaves, and washing machines.

4. Zambians are the most patient people on the planet. My boys can wait eight hours for a court date without batting an eye.

5. Zambian children do not complain or whine, no matter how hungry, hot, or tired they are.

I realized that the children's educational needs should be a priority, and I immediately began homeschooling the children daily. To my disappointment, after paying for the twins to attend private school while they lived at Pastor Bernard's, they had not made any progress and had actually regressed during our eight-month separation. They still did not know the entire alphabet or basic math. Thankfully, I had brought teaching materials to begin the upward climb of teaching the boys how to read. Daily we reviewed basic kindergarten material as the boys struggled to remember elementary skills. Regardless of the lack of educational progress, I was determined not to let that stop me from trying to continue advancing the twins' education.

The cultural differences became more apparent as each day passed. During a school lesson, Victoria asked if we had seen a mermaid in the US. Even after I explained that mermaids were pretend, she could not be convinced otherwise. She was looking forward to spotting one in the US. It did not help that I had a magazine with a picture of a mermaid on it; that was the very confirmation Victoria needed. In addition, she was sure there were dragons to be slain in the US. Victoria anticipated a lot of battles to fight in America.

Village life for the children was vastly different from American culture. The boys dramatically explained in the Bemba language how they used a "slasher" (machete) to kill large snakes and rats. The dreaded poisonous snake, the Black Mamba, had been seen in the village along with other deadly animals. I decided to make a connection between a slasher and reading fluency by trying to retell the incident by drawing pictures.

The Black Mamba is one of the deadliest snakes in the world and it is Africa's largest poisonous snake.

Another cultural difference was that none of the children had ever celebrated a birthday. Since all three were born in September, we decided to celebrate all the birthdays together. At the idea of a party, the kids buzzed with excitement. Purchasing toys was out of the question since the prices were ten times higher than the cost of toys in the US. We walked to a local store, and each child picked out a dry, crumbly pastry. That night we put a large candle in the middle of the pastry, lit it like a torch and sang Happy Birthday at least twenty times. The electricity was out for the fifteenth time, making it a perfect night to hold the celebration.

As part of the adoption process, the children were required to complete physicals. Unbelievably, there were only two doctors in all of Zambia who were certified to give US approved exams. As a result, we knew that it could be a long and arduous process. Since the boys had never gone to a doctor before, we didn't know how they would react to the physical.

HIV prevalence in Zambia is 14.3% (National AIDS Coalition)

After traveling through the city and arriving at the clinic, we found out the doctor was ill and we would have to return at a later time. Knowing that we could not get the visas until the exam was completed, we pressed the issue with the assistant and returned the next day. Our greatest concern was the possibility of the boys being HIV positive. The odds were stacked against them, since their grandmother had HIV and tuberculosis. In addition, their biological parents were assumed to have been positive. Also, Andre did not understand why he had to receive booster shots and needed to be held down by a large Zambian worker. Afterwards we waited several hours while the physicals were completed. We rejoiced when the results came back negative for HIV! We felt a rush of relief and were thankful for God's watchful eye over Andrew and Andre. We also discovered that the boys, who were forty pounds in March, were now sixty-four pounds in November. We figured that the worms had lost the battle!

Since the heat had become unbearable, we took the children to a local pool. To our surprise, there was not a single patron in the Olympic-sized pool. We then found a worker, and he gave us permission to swim. The entrance price was two dollars; it was unfathomable for Zambian families to be able to afford the price. The large pool was more than the boys could ever have imagined. They jumped in with excitement and quickly became accustomed to the water. As I scanned the facility, I did not see any filtration system or chemicals. I wondered if the pool could possibly be a cesspool of parasites; but I then threw all caution to the wind and decided to seek relief from the hot Zambian sun.

Soon, a few local young men joined the fun and attempted to swim. They were all hanging onto the wall looking like the cowardly lion; not one of them was able to swim. It was quite comical as I viewed grown young men hanging on for dear life. To be a Good Samaritan, I offered swimming lessons to one young man. Since life in Zambia consists of hard labor, he had more muscle mass than any body builder in the US. I quickly discovered that muscle sinks and fat floats. Soon I was teaching lessons to the rest of the young men and ladies in the pool. Bathing suits are a luxury and only for the wealthy; therefore, the women wore their underwear, and the men wore their boxers. I was unsure if I was in a Hanes underwear store or in a third world country. After the lesson, to the delight of the young muscleman, he was able to stay afloat and swim across the pool without any help.

That night, as I lay in bed with the mosquito netting gently flowing in the breeze, I contemplated what life in the States would be like for the children. Andrew, Andre, and Victoria had never experienced fresh running water to bathe in. They only had the moonlight to illuminate their hut. It never occurred to them that they were missing a refrigerator in order to grab a bite to eat or get a cool drink. The boys even lacked a soft bed to lay their heads on and a warm blanket to cover them in the chill of the night.

The three of them washed their clothes by the river or in a tub and had no knowledge of a washer or dryer. They had not been exposed to television or other electronics for entertainment. The children sat on a hard floor to eat.

Andrew and Andre's only toy was a car they had made from mud. Instead of having a ball, they attempted to kick an ear of corn to play soccer. The children walked five miles to school without ever thinking about taking a bus or car for transportation. Eating with their fingers without utensils was the norm. Education was a dismal experience for the twins since they had never read a book or held a textbook. Most of all, the three children lacked a mother's love to tuck them in at night. This was normal life in the village for Andrew, Andre, and Victoria.

Victoria was keenly aware of the heartaches Kerry and I were experiencing and our difficulties with the paperwork as she accompanied us to each official appointment. Victoria rejoiced in each victory we had with the adoption process. She started to bond with the boys as they played soccer and games together. Her infectious laugh would light up the room. At times, she would approach me and inquire about American culture. Questions like, "Will I ride a bus to school and wear school uniforms?" and "How will I find the bathrooms at school?" revealed her fears of moving across the world. At times Victoria would have a solemn expression. Wondering if Kerry and I would return to Africa a third time for her adoption, she had doubt etched in her heart.

While I taught the children, Kerry ran from office to office to complete the paperwork for the boys to come to the States. Other days we both worked with officials at the US Embassy, trying to untangle the pages and pages of paperwork. At the embassy, we were treated as a number, and at the time there was little concern for the children. After all, there are over a million orphans in Zambia. After the third visit to the embassy, the official mentioned that we needed the death certificates of the boys' deceased parents. We had affidavits verifying their deaths, but it was not adequate. We disputed the issue back and forth, realizing that it would be nearly impossible to obtain the correct paperwork. Their parents apparently had died within days of each other. Officials speculated that they were infected with HIV or malaria and had died in the village. We knew that it would be nearly impossible to locate the death certificates and were faced with another major roadblock in trying to get the boys out of Zambia.

Kerry and I were on a rabbit trail to find the correct paperwork. There was no record or trace of any evidence regarding the parents' deaths. Kerry sprinted from office to office, and we soon found out that since we were not related to the boys, the certificates were impossible to obtain. We then hired a local official to dig up the paperwork, which became a dead end, and the documents were not recovered. Our last ditch effort was to travel back to the village and meet with the chief to verify the death of their biological parents. Unbelievably, the chief only made appointments on Wednesdays. It was Thursday when we discovered this information, and to our dismay we were running out of time. I sat stunned as Kerry told me the news. We had already been in Zambia for three weeks and could not stay much longer.

The following is an email written to American friends as we struggled to obtain the documents:

November 8, 2011

"Kerry set out early, along with the cook who escorted him, to uncover the long lost death certificate of Victoria's father and the boys' biological parents. On the local bus through the darkest part of town, they went to an obscure clinic, where they were told Victoria's father died. After digging through boxes of files, it was nowhere to be found. Next, onto the morgue that was no bigger than a small room. The cook was freaked by the dead bodies and wanted to run out of the morgue. Once again, the certificate was not found. Lo and behold, after calling Victoria's grandmother, she mentioned he had died at home. We now needed to check at a local hospital. Tomorrow will bring another adventure."

Kerry then tried to navigate by foot to the social welfare office in the capital city of Lusaka. Each set of offices was two miles apart; therefore, it was a grueling trip back and forth to each office. The social welfare office was a long, dark, stifling brick corridor. It reminded me of an old black and white movie of a torture chamber. That, of course, reminded me of our torture. We had been waiting for the document for five days in order to obtain the visas. They had not been processed. Kerry watched the head social worker use an old manual typewriter to finish the document, only to make an error on the date. Not wanting to admit his error, the social worker blamed Kerry for the error, and it took another two hours to complete the application to process birth certificates.

We then raced to the US Embassy, only to be informed that the boys' biological parents' death certificates are needed and that they will not take the signed affidavits from family members. We were unsure where their deceased parents had lived or when and where they died. To exasperate the situation, their grandmother had moved out of the village to another obscure village. But, of course, the officer at the US Embassy assured us that we would be able to obtain the certificates. The officer casually stated that we had to get the document from the chief of the village. I stood in front of the officer with my mouth gaping open in disbelief. Thoughts of trying to find a chief in an obscure village seemed ridiculous to me. I wondered if I should run for chief! Kerry's adventure landed him a doozey of a sunburn on the top of his head. We thought we would have fried eggs cooked on his head in the morning.

I was faced again with the reality of being separated from Andrew and Andre. It was beyond belief that I would leave my adopted boys across the world again. I was stunned by the news. Tears rolled down my face at the prospect of leaving the children across the globe. How could this be the plan of the Lord? Questions of where the boys would go, and who would care for their needs, sent my nurturing instincts sky-rocketing. Facing the inevitable, we called to book a flight for the next morning. We would have to leave without the boys. That morning I cried as I packed the boys' few outfits into their suitcase. I was bewildered, and my tears ran down my face like a dripping faucet. I was tired of trying to be brave and strong. Again, I pleaded with the Lord to deliver the boys. My maternal heart was torn into pieces, and I did not have the strength to pull myself together. I wanted to wrap the boys in my arms and never let them go.

Before leaving the guesthouse, I urged Kerry to make one more desperate effort to contact the US Embassy. We had a dismal chance of reaching the officials since it was Veterans Day and the US Embassy was closed. We were at a dead end. Out of desperation, I decided to email the top official and wait on the slim chance that someone would respond. I simply wrote in the email, 'We were unable to find the death certificates of the deceased parents of the twins. We are flying out in the morning, and we will return the boys to their original state.'

Kerry loaded our suitcases outside. We then began to close the laptop but realized that a new email was in our inbox. Miraculously, within ten minutes a response was given by the top US Embassy official.

It stated, "What do you mean the boys' original state?"

I replied, "Yes, back to the village where they came from." A long pause between emails seemed like an eternity. I realized that the official knew that it would mean a fatal outcome for the boys, who did not have a primary caretaker to meet their basic needs. After dialoguing back and forth, the official declared that a team of officials would privately fly into the village to verify that the boys' parents were actually deceased.

The agent stated, "Don't leave Zambia."

The officials would now have to find an obscure village, a remote hut, and an ailing grandmother in order to gather proper verification. Realizing that the mission was nearly impossible, Kerry and I quickly contacted an IN administrator and Pastor Bernard to alert them that the US Embassy would be descending on the village. Thankfully, they were able to meet the officials and escort them into the village. What a spectacular sight it was! The US Embassy was coming to the desolate Baluba Village and would be confronted with the challenge of trying to dialogue with a non-English speaking grandmother. After the officials arrived at the grandmother's hut, they sat down with the ailing grandmother and a distant uncle in order to verify that the boys were truly orphans. Amazingly, they gathered correct documentation and then flew out of the area to start processing the visas.

After canceling our flight, Kerry and I paced back and forth waiting to hear any pending news. When Kerry's phone rang, he scrambled to answer it.

"Hello, this is Kerry Frantz," he quickly answered. "No way, amazing! The visas have been processed!"

After Kerry hung up the phone we jumped for joy, hugging and rejoicing that the boys will be coming home to America to join our family. I was overwhelmed by God's deliverance of Andrew and Andre. What a miracle it was when Kerry arrived at the embassy and was handed the visas. The boys looked their best, and they were proud as peacocks. The boys knew that they would soon be flying to the US. A joyful celebration took place in the US Embassy with all the officials and our little family. There was a sense of awe and relief as we all realized that the hand of God had come down and rescued Andrew and Andre. Even though we celebrated that night, we had mixed emotions, knowing that we would be leaving Victoria behind once again.

October 20th, 2011, was the day the adoption was finalized for Andre and Andrew Frantz

Chapter 9
Splendor Before Good-bye

Kerry and I wanted to visit somewhere special during our last weekend in Zambia. We decided to travel to Livingston to visit Victoria Falls, the world's largest waterfall and one of the seven wonders of the modern world. The boys, who had never traveled outside of the village, were now on a family vacation! We traveled seven hours in an overcrowded bus, and along the way we encountered potholes the size of elephants. When we arrived at Victoria Falls, we discovered that our traveling adventure was worth it; the falls were spectacular! Surprisingly, few people were in the park because the fee of fifty cents was too much to pay. As we hiked through the trails and started to walk down rocky stairs, the boys trailed behind us, enjoying the view. Once they realized they had fallen behind, they decided to start running down the stairs in order to catch up with us. They had never encountered a flight of stairs before, and, as they descended, their little legs gained momentum; with every stair they gained more speed. Watching their arms flailing in the air and their legs looking like spokes turning on a wheel, I knew I had to stop their faces from becoming a permanent part of the cement and turning into a fossil. Exhilarated by their accelerated speed, the boys were oblivious to the pending danger ahead of them. Instinctively, I braced myself at the bottom of the stairs in order to block their momentum with my body. Like a good soldier, I stood my ground and waited for the impending impact. Andrew decided to abandon the rollercoaster experience and leaped into the air like a gazelle and landed in the bushes. Andre, the less adventurous twin, plowed into me with such velocity that I was catapulted into the air and landed several feet away. I clumsily fell on a thorny bush. When I regained my equilibrium, I started to pick thorns out of my backside. Andre stood there, stunned, not having any idea of what had actually happened. Obviously, the boys did not understand the laws of dynamics. I knew that this was only the beginning of many more surprising situations.

A famous feature of Victoria Falls is the naturally formed Devil's Pool, which sits near the edge of the falls on the Zambian side. When the river flows at a certain level, a rock barrier forms that allows daring swimmers to venture out a few feet from where the water cascades over the falls. We could not resist the temptation to swim in Devil's Pool. Kerry and I had made it thus far with the adoption, so why not experience one more adventure? We waded in the cool refreshing water at the top of the falls. There was a magnificent view of the water descending below us only a few feet away. As we began to climb out of Devil's Pool, a fisherman told us that there were alligators swarming around the body of water. That was all the adventure I wanted to experience!

The Hippopotamus' hide alone can weigh half a ton. It is the third-largest living land mammal.

After our trip, I wanted to fulfill one of my longtime dreams of going on an African safari. Kerry and I decided to hire a taxi driver to take us to a wilderness park. As we drove through the dry arid terrain, the winding dirt roads led us to amazing discoveries. Acacia trees adorned the sculptured landscape. Subtly, we peered in the brush to find a female monkey sitting and gazing curiously at us as she nursed her baby. Around the bend we discovered giraffes pruning the understory branches of acacia trees. Zebras, with their familiar horse-like physique and distinct black and white striping pattern, grazed on the grassland. The hippos were barely noticeable as they were basking in the thick dark mud. The hippopotami had the familiar barrel-shaped torso, along with an enormous mouth and teeth. Another partially submerged hippopotamus tried to keep cool in the hot African sun. I was surprised by their tremendous size when the hippos began to submerge like a submarine under the mud. At the end of our safari, we spotted a herd of elephants basking in the sun near a river. Amazed, we pulled over to view them migrating along the river.

Suddenly, the male leader became protective of the herd and charged us. The taxi driver panicked and yelled for us to get into the vehicle. Narrowly escaping, we jumped into the cab and drove away. When I looked back, the elephants were in a cloud of dust as their trunks sprinkled dirt on their backs.

After we returned from Victoria Falls, we began to pack for our flight. A sense of sorrow came over me with the knowledge that we would be leaving Victoria behind once again. Kerry and I dreaded leaving her, and the finality of our departure settled in like a dark misty cloud. We still did not have a court date for Victoria, and we were well aware that her paperwork was going to end in five short weeks. Victoria's eyes filled with tears as she watched me pack my bags. I sat her on the edge of the bed and took out a childhood ring that I had brought from home. I gave it to her, promising that we would return. It fit her finger perfectly, and I hoped that perhaps it would bring her a small amount comfort. I wondered if we would ever be able to become her parents or if we would ever see her again.

I pleaded with the Lord. "Will You grant us Your grace and allow us to adopt Victoria too?"

My faith seemed weak and restless. My emotions sailed the stormy seas.

Jesus reminded me of the verse that I held so dear: "The Lord is close to the brokenhearted and saves those who are crushed in spirit" (Ps. 34:18). I was comforted that the Lord would watch over and protect Victoria.

The next day I was scheduled to fly to the US, with Kerry, Andrew, and Andre following in a few days. When we arrived at the airport, the boys were confused about the arrangements and Victoria was somber about me leaving. When we approached the ticket counter at seven a.m., we discovered that my plane ticket was never purchased by our travel agent. I was alarmed and shaken that I did not have a flight. This was the last straw for me. The pressure of all the difficulty that we had encountered in Zambia began to crush me like a wrecking ball. I was out of strength, out of courage, and tired of the journey. We had already dealt with the corruption, bribes, lies, and piles of paperwork, and now the thought of not having a flight hit me like a tidal wave. I cried out to the Lord, "Be gracious to me! I beg You to deliver me one more time."

I felt a renewed strength and knew that the Lord was going to help me negotiate another hurdle. Realizing that I had to get back to the US for my other children, I became anxious about getting a flight. With sweat dripping down my back, I raced from one airline to another, begging agents to examine flight schedules. At last, I found a flight; I had ten short minutes to get on board. I then gently turned to Victoria to say good-bye. Unsure if we would ever get a court date for Victoria, I wondered if this would be the last time I would be able to hold her in my arms.

As I hugged her good-bye, I could barely let go of her. Then, as I turned to leave, my phone rang. It was the lawyer; he explained that a court date was set for Victoria. With eight days to spare, it was set for December 22, 2011! It was the Lord's perfect timing, especially since her paperwork expired January 1. Victoria and I laughed and hugged; we would be returning in one month to repeat the arduous adoption process. I ascended up the stairs with tears streaming down my face, thankful that we had one more chance to adopt Victoria. It was a bittersweet departure as I once again waved good-bye to this precious little girl.

After taking Victoria to a local pastor's home, Kerry flew out of Zambia a few days later. The boys had an adventurous plane ride to America. Before meeting us, the twins had never even taken a ride in a car, much less a plane! The boys knew that we were flying to America but never imagined all the amenities on the flight. The food, various buttons to press on the back of the seats, and viewing the clouds out the window were all a fascinating experience for them. The boys peered out the window, wide-eyed and astonished. While sipping soda, the boys asked plenty of questions about the clouds, the sun, and the small cities below. After twenty-five-hours in the air, and with over fifteen hours of sleep, the boys and Kerry finally arrived in Chicago.

The lights, highways, and traffic were all a spectacular scene for the boys. They were amazed by the lights that lined the corridors and were unsure of the escalators at the airport. Kerry jumped onto the first stair of the descending escalator, forgetting that the boys had never encountered moving stairs. After Kerry reached the first floor, he realized that the boys did not follow him. He looked up at the top of the escalator and found them wide-eyed and speechless. Realizing that the boys were left behind, Kerry quickly went back up the adjacent escalator to teach them how to step onto it. The boys proceeded to step onto the first moving stair but failed to hold onto the railing. They were startled when their feet were swept along the descending stairs and their upper bodies leaned backwards. The boys bellowed out laughter as their arms were flailing and their bodies wobbled down the escalator. When the trio exited the terminal, Kerry searched for his ride. Not understanding the rules of the road, the boys immediately stepped out into traffic. Startled by their bold move, Kerry quickly lurched and grabbed them by the collars.

As Andrew and Andre stood outside, they were stunned by the November frigid temperature. It felt like an ice age to them. Andrew and Andre experienced sensory overload as they tried to take in all the sights and sounds of American life. Realizing the boys were hungry, Kerry decided to take them on their first trip to McDonalds. Having no idea what to expect, the boys sat in the restaurant, stunned, and ate their hamburger.

After driving home from O'Hare airport, Kerry finally pulled up into our driveway. The boys anxiously waited to see their new home. When they stepped into the garage, Andrew marveled at the size of our house. He thought the garage was his new home. Andrew and Andre were thrilled as they jumped up and down to see the bikes and scooters in the garage. I had begun to collect secondhand items for the boys, anticipating their arrival. They couldn't be happier. I quickly ushered the twins in the door and our frisky Labradoodle greeted them. "Welcome to America!" Andre announced to the dog. Exhilaration was in the air as the boys scanned the inside of the house.

When the boys rushed into the kitchen, the very first thing they did was to open the refrigerator. As they scanned the contents inside, their mouths dropped open, and relief was on their faces. Wide-eyed and eager, they began to dart from one room to the next, not sure what the function was of each room. Kerry and I took them up to their bedroom, which contained two twin beds. It was more than they imagined, as their eyes carefully searched the room for toys. I prepared a small shoe box of used toys for them. I was careful not to indulge them since it is rare for a Zambian child to even have one toy. They jumped with anticipation as they rummaged through the small box of trinket toys. Andrew and Andre were bubbling over with excitement.

As I tucked the boys into bed that night, I could hardly believe that the boys are part of the Frantz family forever. They rested peacefully in their new beds, basking in the comfort of their new home. Kerry and I were extremely thankful that the Lord had delivered Andrew and Andre from the poverty and evil they were used to living in. Later that night, I checked on the sleeping boys. I chuckled to myself as I saw them huddled on the floor. They were not accustomed to sleeping in a bed. They were wrapped from to head to toe in their blanket to ward off any malaria-infested mosquitoes seeking to bite them. As I carried them back into their beds, I wondered if Andrew or Andre would ever grasp how the Lord had moved mountains to deliver them from impending doom. They were safe now. God had showed His tender hand by caring for His orphans.

The next day it was our priority to introduce the boys to our older children. When Andrew and Andre met their sisters for the first time, they sheepishly grinned at the girls, who were playful with them. Andrew and Andre had difficulty saying their names, Brittany became "Britten," and Bethany became "Bethen." The twins quickly became accustomed to having sisters around and soon tried to communicate using the little English they had acquired. We slowly introduced the twins to other family members, trying to make their adjustment as easy as possible.

Communicating with the boys was a constant challenge. Picture dictionaries and many hand gestures gave the appearance that we played charades all day long. At times, Andre would get frustrated and emphatically wave his arms as he spoke in Bemba. I just stood there dumbfounded, not having a clue what he was saying. Thankfully, Victoria would soon arrive in the US to help translate and close the communication gap.

Trying to maintain balance and a routine in our home was a challenge. Teaching them how to turn faucets on and off, keep outside doors closed, flush toilets, and keep the refrigerator door closed were only a few of our hurdles. The boys tested their finger dexterity as they pushed all the buttons on the microwave, stove, dishwasher, and dryer. Andrew and Andre had to use their problem-solving skills to discover how to squeeze toothpaste from a tube, how to squeeze socks on their feet, how to put a belt through narrow loops, and how to button eight buttons on a shirt. As for me, I had to use my problem-solving skills to keep one step ahead of them and steer them toward healthy activities.

After one week of adjusting, the challenge remained for me to try and get the boys ready for their first day of school. Due to their size and the uncertainty of their age, the administrators agreed that the twins should be placed in third grade. For the first day of school, I was determined to have a successful morning. The night before, I methodically set out clothes, gave baths, and made lunches for everyone. With all the school preparations done, I anticipated that I would have the jump start we needed to be on time for school. The following is a portion of a featured article that was written about how we made the lunches the night before.

> *Time to get ready for school.*

> *Nancy Frantz begins to teach the twins how to prepare their lunches. She announces eagerly, "Let's make a sandwich!"*

Zambians don't make sandwiches. So Nancy tries to explain the concept of a sandwich as part of a how-to lesson. As she talks, she hands a piece of bread to Andrew, while Andre asks how beans - he really likes beans - fit into the equation. As she begins to discuss proper sandwich options with Andre, she looks back at Andrew, who is gobbling his bread.

"No," she says. "That is for your sandwich." She pulls deli cuts of meat from the fridge. She chirps, "Make your sandwiches."

The brothers grab the meat, look at each other, and then toss slices into their lunch boxes. "No," she says, again, "the meat is for your sandwiches."

They get the sandwiches assembled, then it's time to wrap them. Nancy tells them to use a baggie, and the pair crack up. No reason, except "baggie" - they have no idea what a baggie is - simply sounds funny to them.

Nancy begins to show them how to insert the sandwich into the baggie, and then seal the top. Plop. Sandwich falls to the ground. The dog begins to rush over, but Nancy plucks it up in the nick of time.

She blows dirt off Andre's sandwich—no way they're going to restart the whole rigmarole this morning - and slips it into a bag.

Meanwhile, she spots Andrew putting his sandwich away—into the towel drawer. Slam, dunk.

With no benefit in frustration, she opts for amusement. Grinning, she whispers to herself, "Mission accomplished."

(Phil Luciano)

The alarm rang at six a.m., and the morning marathon started; I was determined to be on time for the first day of school. Due to the frigid December air, the boys had to wear items they were not accustomed to. It became apparent that they had to tackle too many zippers, buttons, and snaps. I knew that I had missed a teaching moment when Andrew came out dressed with his underwear over his pants and his shirt on backwards. Never having put on gloves before became a new challenge for Andrew and Andre. Putting each individual finger in each hole was a mountain I did not want to climb. Stuffing their hand into the gloves gave the appearance that they were fingerless; I then snatched up their backpacks and loaded the car. Having never worn a seatbelt, the boys were confused and baffled about which strap went where. And, of course, not having any fingers made it an impossible task. I let out a sigh and glanced at my watch; it was 7:30, we had five minutes before school began.

We quickly pulled up to the school and I told the boys, "It is time for your first day of school. Unbuckle your seatbelts."

The boys sat there frozen in time; they did not know what the word "unbuckle" meant, much less how to do it. Andre decided that the task was too difficult and tried to escape without actually unbuckling his seatbelt. As he opened the door, he made a mad dash to get out of the car and flipped upside down, then dangled outside in the frigid air. He was wrapped up, tangled, and tousled without ever stepping outside of the car. Hearing the school bell, I frantically tried to untangle the mess and flipped him upright. I finally managed to get the boys out of the car. I was exhausted, and the day was just beginning.

Wanting to be the perfect mom, I snatched my camera out of my pocket and said, "Smile, boys, this is your first day of school!"

A stark contrast between American and Zambian schools became immediately apparent to Andrew and Andre. Sadly, they were at least four years behind their American counterparts. The largest contrast between the educational systems is the way teachers treat their students. In Zambia, the boys were beaten several times simply for arriving late after walking miles to school. The slightest infraction, such as talking, would bring severe punishment. When I told the boys that teachers in American cannot beat students, and if they do hurt a student, the teacher would go to jail, the boys laughed at the thought, thinking how ridiculous it was that America would have such a law.

Winter was a new experience for the twins. Early one school morning, the boys woke up to snow on the ground. At six a.m. they were ecstatic when they cracked opened the back door. Andrew and Andre did not realize that snow was cold; consequently, they ran out into the snow with bare feet. They immediately danced and hopped in the snow to avoid the new sensation of being cold. Then they encountered the best discovery of all. Snow can actually be made into a ball and be thrown at each other. They did not understand the law of physics that snow belongs outside in cold temperatures. As a result, they brought the fun inside by throwing snowballs that were plastered on the walls and furniture. A snowball fight arose in the house, and the boys were squealing and buzzing with energy. Walking on ice was a new concept for the African children. They slipped and slid with arms and legs flying in all directions. I was exhausted, and it was only 6:30 a.m.!

Another challenge was their diet and nutrition. To prevent their digestion system from going into overdrive I slowly introduced new foods into their diet. With their new diet, Andrew and Andre were rapidly growing and gaining weight. In Zambia, at the age of eleven, the boys weighed thirty-nine pounds, which is equivalent to the weight of a three-year-old in America. The twins were growing an inch a month and reached the weight of sixty-two pounds. They craved potassium and protein, and each day they ate more than a man. The boys would daily consume ten bananas and eight pieces of bread. This was a stark contrast to when they were in Zambia, when the twins would catch birds with their hands and eat them to fill their stomachs. Also, American food was far different from the fried caterpillars and termites they used to consume for protein. While in Zambia, if Andrew and Andre felt ill, they would eat the clay soil to fill their stomachs, believing this would heal them. Survival meant taking desperate measures.

In Zambia, Andrew and Andre never had rich or sweet foods; therefore, they became fascinated by all the treats in the US. One day at the supermarket the boys begged for the "big white clouds," which, in fact, were marshmallows. Reluctantly, I bought them, and when we arrived at home their hands frantically rummaged through the bags for the "clouds." The bag was ripped open; as they consumed the marshmallows, they gagged and choked them out into the garbage.

One night I made Jell-O and gave each boy a bowlful. It was clearly a foreign substance for them. Attracted to the bright color but uncertain about the texture, the boys cautiously investigated the bowl. They continued to jiggle and jostle the Jell-O. They laughed as they talked about the word Jell-O and how silly it sounded. The boys then proceeded to take the plunge and put a spoonful in their mouth. Their eyes widened, not knowing if they should chew it, spit it out, or swallow it whole. After they digested the foreign substance, they both decided that it was too "sweetie" for them and they would rather stick with bananas.

As each day passed, Andrew and Andre became more accustomed to their new family. One morning Andre was sitting and eating breakfast when he somberly said, "Zambia bad, America good."

At that moment, I wanted to communicate to Andre that although the Zambians endure much suffering, God cares for them too. I knew that Andre would not understand, so I hugged him and said it was okay to feel that way. Andrew and Andre were tucking away the memories of their suffering and moving forward with their new life in America.

Chapter 10
The Eleventh Hour

With each passing day, Kerry and I missed Victoria and her sweet smile more. When we spoke with her on the phone, we discovered that she was counting down the days until our arrival. As a result of our financial support for Victoria, she was able to attend a private school. Slowly she began to improve her English and was able to hold a conversation with us. Unfortunately, similar to her teachers in the village, her instructors were also harsh and administered ruthless discipline. Victoria, naturally compliant by nature, strove to please her teachers by being diligent in her studies. Even though she lived in the pastor's home, where her needs were met, she continued to struggle with the many transitions in her life. Victoria had been tossed from one caretaker to another, changed schools, left her village behind, and now tried to adjust to a new family. These challenges were difficult for her. At times, she became sullen and withdrew from her foster family. My heart broke for her emotional well-being, and I wanted to be there for her. I felt like a mother hen wanting to gather her chicks. Kerry and I both felt the urgency to go to Zambia and take care of her.

Wanting it check on Victoria's well-being, I spoke with her by phone and asked her how her schooling was going. Casually, I asked her about the ring that I gave her. She lowered her voice and explained what happened at school. "Girls are not allowed to wear jewelry at school and I forgot to take off the ring when I got to class. The teacher called me up to the front of the class when he saw the ring on my finger. He asked me where I got the ring and why I was wearing it in school. I told him that my mom gave it to me."

"Oh no" I said apprehensively. "What happened next?"

There was a long pause on the phone. "The teacher had gotten mad and then he called me in front of the class. He then brought out a pipe and beat me."

I gasped and was alarmed. "Did anything else happen besides the beating?" I inquired.

"Yes", Victoria whispered, "I had to dig a ditch for five days in the hot sun."

"How could this happen since we have placed you in a private school?" I said with anger in my voice. "What happened to the ring?"

Victoria despondently stated, "He took it and never gave it back".

The situation caused me to fight harder to rescue her from her plight.

At home my biological children were involved in the process of the adoption and prayed daily for Victoria to become part of our family. Our fifteen-year-old adopted daughter, Brittany, was also invested in the adoption. She sold bracelets, helped with a fundraiser, and wrote letters to Victoria. It was amazing how the Lord was working on the hearts of all our children to make us one growing family.

November quickly passed, and Kerry and I were scheduled to fly to Zambia on December 18, trying one last time to adopt Victoria. Preparing for our third trip to Zambia in nine months was like gearing up to climb a mountain. We understood that the orphans in Baluba Village continued to lack food and clothing and were in desperate need. Before we left, we were able to collect extra funds to use for another food distribution. My heart ached for the babies with bulging bellies and hollow eyes, and we wanted to provide for their basic needs.

It also became my passion to collect three hundred pairs of used shoes for the orphans. At midnight before an early flight, I encountered the challenge of stuffing three-hundred pairs of used shoes in six oversized suitcases. Knowing that each pair would be a priceless possession to the orphans, I became obsessed about squeezing every last shoe into each pocket. The mission was accomplished, and we wearily zipped up the last suitcase. Kerry and I then quickly packed a carry-on of all of our personal belongings for the long trip across the world.

Having to leave the boys in America after only three weeks of family bonding was emotionally difficult for me. Nevertheless, they understood the importance of our trip and wanted Victoria to join our family. We were faced again with trying to find them a temporary home while Kerry and I were in Zambia. We knew it would be a challenge since we did not know how long we would be gone, and the boys did not speak any English. Eventually, Kerry's sister graciously offered to take care of the boys while we were gone. With Victoria's paperwork expiring January 1, Kerry and I knew that the deadline for her adoption was fast approaching. We had one last chance to get Victoria out of Zambia and only fourteen days to successfully navigate a corrupt government. If the adoption failed, Victoria would have to return to the village and once again face extreme poverty.

After a twenty-hour flight, we landed in South Africa. We had twenty hours before our court appointment, and we had to take two additional flights in order to arrive in Ndola. After we rushed to take the flight out of South Africa, we stood in line to board a bus that connected us to the correct airline. The temperature was hot and muggy; sweat dripped down Kerry's face while we gathered the correct paperwork.

Staring directly into Kerry's eyes, the attendant emphatically asked, "Do you have your yellow fever forms?" Kerry and I looked at each other in disbelief, never having been informed that we needed a yellow fever shot to leave South Africa. I was stunned. The court time was only twenty hours away, and I was well aware that we were still two countries away from Zambia. My pulse began to rise, and I felt a rush of panic. My motherly instincts bubbled over like a volcano, and I knew I had to act quickly. Instinctively, I crouched down, grabbed the briefcase filled with the adoption papers, and proceeded to duck past the counter. I made a mad dash, running for the bus, jostled my way onto it, and burrowed myself in the center of the crowd. With a slight glance over my shoulder, I noticed that Kerry's arms were flailing as he tried to explain his way out of the situation. I was going to get to court no matter what, even if Kerry had to stay behind in South Africa! On the bus, people were pressing around me and began to notice that I was hiding from the officials. The rays from the hot sun were beating down on the bus, and it was like a pressure cooker ready to pop its lid. As sweat rolled down my temples, one young man asked why I was so frantic.

Whispering, I replied, "We don't have a yellow fever form, and the flight attendant is going to ban us from the flight."

He looked at me in shock, saying in an aggravated tone, "I had a white copy of my yellow fever shot, and they isolated me for six hours because it was not a yellow piece of paper. Lady, you will never get on the plane!!!"

I retorted back, "I was never informed of the yellow fever shot. I am on a mission, and I have to get to Zambia by tomorrow morning."

The man looked incredulously, asking, "You mean missionaries don't get yellow fever?!"

By now I wanted to deck the guy, and I said flatly, "Who needs a smart aleck right now?"

I then glanced past the crowd on the bus and noticed that the flight attendant was now pointing at the bus; I had obviously been discovered. The attendant was now in a dilemma with two options left. Either she drags me off the bus with me yelling about a deadline for a court date, which would inevitably delay hundreds of people on the bus, or she could allow us to board the plane without the yellow fever form. I could see her weighing the options as my husband desperately tried to reason with her. At last, she resigned herself to the situation by allowing Kerry and me to continue our journey without the forms. A sense of relief washed over me like a cool breeze, and at that moment I realized that the Lord had rescued me once more. A familiar verse came to mind, "Fear not, for I have redeemed you; I have called you by name, you are mine. When you pass through the waters, I will be with you; and through the rivers, they shall not overwhelm you; when you walk through the fire you shall not be burned, and the flame shall not consume you. For I am the Lord your God, the Holy One of Israel, your Savior" (Isa. 43:1-3).

Kerry and I then made a mad dash off the bus to board the plane. After getting settled, an argument broke out about the food that was to be served during the flight. South Africans were yelling at each other, and tempers flared about who would be providing the food on the plane. I could not have cared less if I ate anything; I just desperately wanted to get to Zambia. We could not afford any further delay. After several hours of waiting, cheese sandwiches were served on a napkin. I sat back in the seat, peering out the window, anxiously waiting to see Victoria.

The sun was warm on our faces as we exited the plane and began to frantically search for Victoria. High barbed wire fences surrounded the small airport, and armed men were standing guard as we exited. Realizing that we were the only white couple on the entire grounds, I figured Victoria would easily find us first. Behind the barbed wired fence, I heard a voice calling, "Mom! Mom!" and I quickly directed my gaze toward her.

There before me stood a beautiful young lady dressed in brightly adorned clothes. As she smiled broadly, her dimples added to her bright countenance. At that moment, I realized we were not adopting the young girl we first encountered eight months ago but a blossoming young lady. As we left the terminal, we conversed about school, her new family, and how happy we were to finally be reunited. That night the three of us settled into a small guesthouse, and I enjoyed chatting with Victoria over a cup of tea. I lay in bed that night, wondering if the Lord would continue to be gracious to us by allowing us to adopt Victoria. We were at the final hour, and this was the last court appointment. As I drifted off to sleep, I rested in God's goodness and trusted in His promise that He had prepared a future filled with hope.

The following morning brought excitement as we approached the nine a.m. court date. Victoria looked striking, even with her extremely short hair that was required for school. The clothes we brought fit her perfectly, and the floral skirt accented her slim figure. Victoria understood that this day would change her life forever. If the judge granted the adoption, she would become part of the Frantz family. If the judge delayed his decision by even one day, she would be forced to return to the village—never able to become part of our family. With only one day left before the US paperwork expired, we were acutely aware that time had run out; we had one last chance to adopt Victoria.

As we waited outside the courtroom with Pastor Bernard and Medica, we chatted about the long and arduous adoption process. We sat, nervously waiting to be called in by the court official. Victoria sat poised on the bench, glancing over at me with an engaging smile. This was the day we were all waiting for. The sun shone down the small, open corridor as we nervously discussed what court would entail. An official abruptly entered the small hallway and motioned for Kerry, Victoria, the lawyer, and me to wait by the judge's chambers. We were silent as we entered the chambers. Surprisingly, the small room had an air conditioner. It was the first place in Zambia I had ever been that had air conditioning. Kerry, Victoria, and I sat across from the judge who did not even glance at us. He shuffled our papers, leaned back in his chair, and let out a low grunt. It was apparent that the judge was having a bad day and was not at all in the mood to deal with an adoption petition. He then asked Victoria in a low, dark tone, "Do you want to be adopted?" Victoria shyly smiled and said, "Yes."

I squeezed Victoria's hand to reassure of our love for her. The judge then turned his attention to Kerry and questioned him. I nervously squirmed in my seat and dared not look up for fear of jeopardizing the case.

The judge squinted, glaring at Kerry, then proceeded to ask, "How will you be able to provide for seven children on your salary?" Ironically, Kerry's basic salary would be enough to support an entire village in Zambia. I sat quietly, diligently praying for God's mercy to be poured down on us. The judge picked up a pen and with a quick sweep signed the adoption papers. We had to remain still and quiet, even though I wanted to leap ten feet in the air with excitement! As we left the judge's chambers, exhilaration was in the air, and we quickly hugged and embraced Victoria. We were the new parents of a bouncing fifteen-year-old girl!

Victoria was ecstatic and smiled contently as she stated her new name to the clerk: "Victoria Blessing Frantz."

I marveled at God's perfect timing and how He had written His own signature on the adoption papers. No amount of human effort could have had the slightest chance of adopting three children from Zambia. God moved mountains and parted the Red Sea for three obscure orphans: Andrew, Andre, and Victoria. Sixteen orphans were adopted in all of Zambia in 2011, and three of them became part of the forever-Frantz family. Glory be to God, our Deliverer and Defender of orphans.

Chapter 11
Adopting a Village

The night of the adoption we had a celebration, and I tried to explain what life in America would be like.

Victoria's questions were simple, but direct. "Will I walk to school?", "Who will help me with my homework?", and "How do you get a locker open?" As I answered the questions as simply as possible, I was reminded of the cultural gap that Victoria would be facing when she arrived in America.

On December 22, Kerry had to travel to Lusaka to complete the visa paperwork before the US deadline of December 31. Meanwhile, I remained at the guesthouse with Victoria to fulfill our mission of providing food and shoes for the 350 orphans in the village. Prior to the distribution, I had to retrieve my lost luggage from the small airport in Ndola. I needed to regain the six suitcases that contained the treasured shoes for the orphans. As Bernard and I traveled to the airport, we casually chatted about Victoria's adoption. We did not anticipate any problems with the paperwork and felt confident that we could recover the suitcases. The airport was a small building about the size of a McDonald's. Pastor Bernard and I entered and stood behind the counter, waiting for the armed soldiers to hand us our luggage. We cautiously watched as three soldiers opened each suitcase. The soldiers stood over them, then paused and whispered to one another. My heart sank because I knew how desperately the orphans needed the shoes. The soldiers jumped to the conclusion that the shoes would be sold on the black market. Pastor Bernard and I argued our cause, explaining that we were taking the shoes to the village, but they remained suspicious of our motives.

We were next ushered into the administrator's office. She did not appear to believe our story, emphatically stating, "You will be charged for the shoes." I was aghast about the demanded payment and stood there speechless. Trying to convince her was like trying to convince a judge to change a final verdict. I pleaded with the administrator by explaining: "I have already paid five hundred and forty dollars so that the shoes would safely get to Ndola." Pastor Bernard and I both pleaded with her to waive the charge. I said, "If I give you money for the bags, then I will have less money for food for the orphans."

The agent quickly retorted, "Render to Caesar what is Caesar's."

"But the shoes are donated for the cause of Christ, and render to God what is God's," I passionately replied.

"No." She sneered. "You must RENDER!"

I locked eyes with her, and a verse immediately came to mind. I resolutely said, "And you should not only look out for your own interest but also the interest of others." Without flinching, she firmly held out her hand for payment. I counted out the money that I had set aside for the orphans' food, laid it on her desk, and then abruptly turned to leave her small office.

As I rounded the corner, one of the soldiers grabbed my arm to pull me back into her office. Sweat beaded on my brow as thoughts of being thrown into a Zambian jail were quite unappealing. When I faced the official, she never made eye contact. Amazingly, she proceeded to slap the money back into my hand. In that split second, I knew that the Hounds of Heaven had worked on her heart. As I left her office, I was mindful of the verse that says God is "a Father to the Fatherless," and I knew that He was watching over the needs of the orphans.

The following day, December 23, we prepared for the distribution of the food and shoes in the village. It was the largest distribution in the history of IN Network. We were giving out three thousand pounds of cornmeal, beans, shoes, and gospel books. I knew that the orphans would be hungry, as they would have to wait for hours in the hot sun for their food; therefore, I wanted to also provide sandwiches for the children. Victoria thought it was an extravagance and giggled at the prospect of giving 350 peanut butter sandwiches to the hungry orphans. Victoria and I piled into the pick-up truck driven by a representative from IN Network and drove to the food supply warehouse to load a semi-truck with cornmeal.

When we drove up to the warehouse, the sight of 250 bags of cornmeal, each weighing sixty pounds, was a magnificent sight. As Zambian workers loaded each bag on their shoulders, their heads were getting covered with cornmeal, and the task appeared exhausting. While we were waiting, a crippled man passed by us in a handcrafted wheelchair. He was using his arms to push wooden pedals that moved the wooden wheels forward. When I asked him where he had received the wheelchair, he proudly said that a missionary made it for him. Even though I felt pity for the disabled man, I realized that God had provided for him.

My attention next switched to the loaded truck, and we began to drive toward the village. Winding roads with potholes larger than the truck made for a rough beginning. Sitting in the truck, I knew that the task before us was larger than life. I wished that Kerry was with me to share in the huge task ahead, but I knew that we had to continue to forge forward with the adoption. I prayed for guidance and strength as I faced a village with great needs. As we entered the village, dust hovered over the truck like a dark, looming cloud. Children began to cheer as they ran alongside the truck. Victoria knew many of the children, and her face lit up as we greeted each one of them. Our goal was to quickly unload the supplies, match the shoes, and bag the beans. The distribution building was a small, non-ventilated building that barely had room to contain all the supplies. There were over 350 pairs of stinky shoes, 18 helpers, and 3,000 pounds of cornmeal to fit inside the rustic building.

I brought foot charts from the US so we could measure the orphans' feet to match the size of the shoes. Trying to train the women of the village to size the orphans' feet became a challenging task! After several demonstrations on how to measure the size of a person's foot, the women stared at me like I was from another planet. I grabbed Pastor Bernard's eight-year old English-speaking daughter and quickly explained the procedure. She was then ready to take charge of the shoe sizing ordeal.

Following this training to match the shoes, I wanted to begin the presentation of the Gospel. Outside, Pastor Bernard gathered the children and adults to hear the Good News that Christ could bring hope to their lives. We handed out booklets of the Gospel of John to the adults and children's tracts to the orphans. Sadly, there were more orphans than tracts, which brought disappointment to the children who did not receive one. There was a hush over the crowd as I began to share Christ's love with them. I looked out into the crowd, and my heart broke for their pain and suffering. Not one of the children was smiling or laughing; silence, along with hopelessness, permeated their faces. I was told by Pastor Bernard that, in the crowd of over three hundred people, there were many prostitutes, women so desperately hungry that they would sell their bodies for a meal.

"Lord, have mercy on these dear people," I earnestly prayed.

As the Lord gave me the privilege to speak Bible verses into their hearts, a sweet silence swept over the crowd. They hungered for the Word of God. At the conclusion of the Gospel presentation, I prayed aloud the sinner's prayer. As Pastor Bernard translated the prayer, the crowd repeated it in the Bemba language. It was the most pivotal moment in my Christian life. I looked into the eyes of the children. They were intently listening and soaking in every word that was spoken. As I recited the sinner's prayer, sounds of sweet sincere voices reached heaven with their heartfelt prayers. Afterwards, not one tract or book was left behind or thrown on the ground. The people treasured the Word of God as they intently examined the pictures in the tract.

While I prepared for the distribution, the women helpers would call each child's name to enter the building and get fitted for shoes. It was a chaotic scene, as helpers were barely able to use the shoe-sizing chart. The children did not have a clue what the odd drawing of the foot actually meant. Lifting dirty feet up and down and trying to get their heel lined up was like moving a peg leg! Hour after hour we fitted young children for shoes. If a proper size was unavailable, the child desperately tried to put on a shoe that was too small. Children were waiting for hours outside the building, quietly listening for their name to be called.

One particular fourteen-year-old girl who was on the coveted list was an orphan who had five other siblings. She not only took care of her younger siblings, including a baby, but she was also deaf. I looked deeply into her hollow eyes, seeing the anguish and suffering etched on her young face. I wanted to wrap my arms around her and care for her. The young girl's burden of feeding five other siblings was insurmountable.

"Lord," I pleaded, "Show Your mercy to her and pour out Your grace." The young deaf girl exited the building with new shoes for herself and two of her siblings, one on each hip.

Victoria worked tirelessly, trying to fit shoes on the orphans, distributing sandwiches, and taking care of babies. She quietly talked to her friends from the village and now realized the chasm that existed between her and her orphaned friends. Victoria would secretly slip her clothes to her friends as she was moved by compassion to meet their dire needs. She was gracious to her friends, trying to ease their suffering by giving them some of her possessions. The dramatic change that had occurred in Victoria's life over the past few months was quite evident. She remembered the time when she also stood in the distribution line—hungry, needing rice to fill her empty stomach.

During the distribution, six-year old orphans were given shoes, a sandwich, and a sixty-pound bag of cornmeal. After they received their stipend, children had to drag their bag of cornmeal across the floor and down a large step. Their determination for survival was amazing, and I watched the children do whatever they could to get their bag of cornmeal to their huts.

As the afternoon wore on, the small community building became increasingly stuffy and unbearably warm. I went to a window to get a breath of fresh air and regain my strength. I looked down to see two small children reaching up to the window. I recognized from their little faces that they were Victoria's cousins. Without delay, I motioned for them to go around to the entrance of the building to receive food. As the two children ran for the door, the village ladies who were helping with the distribution abruptly chased them away.

"Wait, wait," I said, "I want them to receive food and shoes!" The ladies flatly stated, "They are not on the list. They do not have a sponsor from America. They cannot receive the food; if they do, then a hundred more orphans in the village will come for food."

Ignoring the warning, with one quick sweep I grabbed one of the young cousins by the arm and pulled him into the building. I could not reach the small girl, and sadly, she was left behind. I handed the barefooted eight-year old boy a sandwich then frantically began to rummage through the shoes to find a pair that fit him. Women stood over me like clucking hens, rebuking me for giving away food that I purchased and shoes that I brought from America. At last, I sent him on his way with the goods. When I looked out the window, I saw him happily run to his hut, wearing his bright new shoes while his sister proceeded to walk away with her head down.

I sat quietly on the bench, exhausted and overcome by the desperate needs of the children. Their gaunt faces, glazed-over eyes, parched lips, torn clothes, dusty legs, and extended bellies shattered my heart into a million pieces. Thoughts of my American home flashed before me. I remembered times of throwing away leftovers, tossing away shoes, spending money on frivolous junk, buying specialty coffee, and owning two vehicles. My possessions were more than the orphaned children could even imagine.

The following is an email I sent back to the States:

"Imagine yourself in a small, non-ventilated building, with three hundred and fifty pairs of stinky shoes, eighteen helpers, three thousand pounds of cornmeal, beans, and, yes, three hundred sandwiches. Now imagine three hundred and fifty orphans waiting at the door, pressing to get a peek, as I try to explain to the Zambian helpers how to use a food sizing chart. You would think that I had introduced an algebraic equation. Then the children come in, three at a time, to get fitted, which becomes a crazy scene. Now I have helpers barely able to use the shoe sizing chart, and children not having a clue what that funny drawing of a foot on paper is, and they have no idea where to put their heel. Unfortunately, Zambians have bigger feet than expected, and I was short fifty pairs of larger shoes. It was heartbreaking, especially since I had little resources left, and shoes cost about fifty dollars a pair in Zambia."

I asked myself, "Was there ever a time I was thankful for fresh water and electricity?" All my material goods seemed small and insignificant in light of the suffering of these little ones. I realized that God had placed in my heart a privileged glimpse of the Father's love for His orphans.

Trying to shake off extreme fatigue, I walked to the door to assess how many orphans were still waiting at the entrance. I estimated about forty tired and hungry orphans that remained waiting in the hot Zambian sun. When I counted the shoes, I noticed that the remaining shoes were much too small for the adolescents waiting outside. The children had been waiting hour upon hour for the shoes, and now I had to inform them that they would not be receiving any. I quickly whispered to Medica our difficult predicament. With sadness in her eyes, she hesitantly walked to the entrance of the building and in the Bemba language explained the disappointing news. A hush settled over the crowd, but not one child moved away from the door. They stood there with disappointment written on their faces. Their eyes revealed their life stories. It was salt in their wounds. This was a way of life for the children, enduring disappointments and heartaches during their short lives. As I looked into their sorrowful eyes, I could barely take in their disappointment. My thoughts raced back to when I was stuffing all the shoes in the suitcases. I wondered why I did not try to stuff a few more pairs inside my purse. I sat quietly on the bench, trying to take in their disappointment. Sadly, I realized that there was no way I could meet the needs of the rest of the orphans. The donations were depleted. I was brought to my knees, begging God to meet the needs of the rest of the orphans.

Pastor Bernard quietly approached me, sensing my bewilderment, and then beckoned me to join him to examine the project that Grace Presbyterian Church sponsored. In order to establish on-going food for the children in the village, a chicken farm had been developed. Walking along a winding path, we traveled to an open field. When we finally arrived at our destination, we entered an elongated building. Inside were hundreds of baby chicks, swarming around my ankles. Lights were suspended from the ceiling to keep them warm. In the corner of the building was a small, meek-looking man wearing a white coat. He was the "chicken man" who nurtured and fed the chicks. He even slept with them! A sigh of relief rushed over me as it gave me a glimmer of hope that continuing food would be provided for the orphans.

When we returned to the village, Medica was sweeping up the floor of the distribution center. Not one bean or pair of shoes was left. The sun began to set, and it was time to leave the precious children. We loaded the empty suitcases into the back of a pick-up, hopped in the bed of the truck, and drove past hut after hut. We passed young children sitting on top of sixty-pound bags they were unable to drag to their huts. I wondered how the little children would be able to get their food home. I sat back in my seat, utterly exhausted, and watched the sun set over the horizon. I marveled at the beauty of the landscape with arcadia trees extending their branches as if pointing to the One in heaven. Peace engulfed me as I closed my eyes and rested under the mighty wings of the Lord.

The largest distribution in the history of the village: 350 pairs of shoes and 50 pounds of cornmeal for each orphan was donated

Chapter 12
Home Sweet Home

We said good-bye to our Zambian friends Billiant, Pastor Bernard, and Medica. We realized that it was the last time we would all be together. Pastor Bernard, who chose Andrew and Andre from the village, was a continual source of guidance and support. Kerry and I would be eternally grateful for their help and care for the children. We would continue to support the food distributions to the orphans in the village, along with the physical needs of Pastor Bernard's family.

After parting ways, Victoria and I took a bus to the capital city, Lusaka. As we were loading the bus, a young man wearing a suit jumped onto the bus. Loudly and clearly he explained the Gospel in the Bemba language to all the passengers. I sat in my seat wide-eyed and amazed as I watched him pace up and down the aisle, carrying an antique, oversized children's Bible. I longed to be able to give him a Bible, but I had given them all away. I prayed a silent prayer for this bold young man that the Lord would provide a Bible for him.

After the preacher hopped off the bus, I noticed that women in adjacent seats were inspecting the contents of my purse. One woman began to inquire about the Tylenol lying on top of my purse.

"What is that bottle for?" inquired the lady.

"It is for when you do not feel well or have a headache," I explained quietly.

Our conversation evoked more questions from several women on the bus. The longing in their eyes for the medicine was evident. Efficiently, I counted out the Tylenol and divided up the pills to give to the women. I was glad that I was able to provide a little relief to their hard lives. Seeking rest, I peered out the bus window and reflected on the arduous journey we had traveled through the adoption process. It was apparent that God's hand had moved insurmountable obstacles to deliver our three children. Peace surrounded me like a soft blanket, and I rested in God's goodness. My rest was short-lived, since we pulled into the bus station late that night. I knew that I had to prepare myself for the bedlam outside the bus doors. Clutching Victoria's hand, we exited the bus, searching for Kerry. As a tall white woman, I became a target for local taxi drivers to swarm around me like flies. Feeling a tug on my elbow, followed by great relief, I realized that Kerry had found Victoria and me. Swiftly, we moved through the crowd and jumped in a taxi to find solace at our guesthouse. That night our little family laughed and talked about what American life would be like for Victoria.

The next day, I booked a flight to travel back to the US, knowing that the boys needed stability at home. Kerry and Victoria would stay behind to finalize the paperwork. At the airport, it was a sweet farewell as I said good-bye to Victoria. As I hugged her, I was relieved that our departure was not like the previous ones. Victoria and I did not shed any tears, and we were thankful that we would see each other in America in one week.

Later, after I had arrived home, on Christmas Day 2011, Kerry sent me this email:

"This Christmas was going to be the loneliest one on record due to no gatherings with friends or family except for the two remaining Frantzes, who will welcome any homecooked meal at this point. For Victoria, who has never received a Christmas present except for a food item, it will be a familiar situation to her. As I contemplate the effort involved in returning to Zambia for a third time in ten months, and now having adopted a fifteen-year-old, I am reminded of the far greater cost Christ paid to leave the glory of heaven and subject Himself to the sorrow and tears of this life. In addition, when looking at the horror He endured for being the sin-bearer to purchase our pardon, I am brought to a deeper appreciation of this real rescuing that makes the Frantz intervention and rescuing of three Zambians pale in comparison. Jesus is the real hero."

After reading Kerry's email, I realized the adoption experience had impacted both of us spiritually in a profound way.

When Kerry obtained the visa for Victoria from the US embassy, a second celebration took place with the head officials. Everyone realized it was miraculous that three children were adopted from Zambia. The visa was processed on December 29, 2011, and her paperwork expired January 1, 2012. The Lord had delivered Victoria just in time!

During the flight to America, Victoria was intrigued by the movies, food, and amenities. It was hard for her to fathom how vastly different it would be from village life. After the twenty-five-hour flight, she was ready to enter her new life. When they arrived, it was overcast, cold, and cloudy in the Windy City, and the weather felt foreign to her. As Victoria stepped out of the airport, she was greeted by a cold northwest wind.

"Whew," Victoria whistled, "The air is so cold." The only heat that Victoria had ever experienced was from the sun. "Why is the air cold outside, but still warm inside?" she inquisitively asked Kerry.

After Kerry and Victoria hopped into the car, she peered out the window, taking in all the sights and sounds of Chicago. Since Victoria had never traveled on an expressway before, she was astounded by all the traffic.

When they pulled into our driveway, I wondered how Victoria would respond to her new home. Wide-eyed and excited, Victoria anxiously entered through the kitchen. Similar to Andrew's and Andre's reaction, she immediately went to the refrigerator.

"Wow, food!" she announced, excited.

As I led her to each room, she scanned the contents and smiled from ear to ear. Then I ushered Victoria into her bedroom, and she looked excitedly at the contents of her closet. Victoria could barely contain her enthusiasm as we finished the tour of her new home. I asked her, "What do you like best about your new home?" With a smile on her face that could light up a Christmas tree, she said, delighted, "EVERYTHING!" That night, on December 31, after all the children were tucked into bed, I marveled at the Lord's amazing timing. The Lord was ushering in the New Year with the completion of the Frantz family.

Chapter 13
Life in America

Establishing a routine in the US became a challenge for the Frantz family. Even though I had taught the boys how to tell time, a schedule did not have any relevance to the children. One day, as I drove her to school, Victoria stated matter-of-factly, "You Americans use your wrist to find out the time; in Zambia, we used the sun to know what time it was."

Fortunately, a missionary had helped us understand that Zambians think in a circular manner. She explained that most Africans live each day with the challenge of gathering enough food and water to sustain a person for a single day. If an African had enough food, then it was a good day, and the cycle would begin all over again in the morning. With American culture, most people have a linear time schedule with sequential events and accomplished plans throughout the week. Consequently, even though the boys knew how to tell time, it did not have any relevance to them. As a result, every day became a challenge as I tried to raise an awareness of a schedule. The boys were oblivious to what year, month, and day it was, instead enjoying and living for each moment. When Andrew and Andre woke up each morning, they were happy there was food for the day, and then they would go play without a worry or care in the world.

Each day we worked on building their English skills and often found ourselves in the international Twilight Zone! This is a typical conversation that would be heard in our household. Andrew, who is naturally inquisitive, asked what a proper noun was. He apparently heard his teacher speak on the topic.

Victoria, who just happened to be studying proper nouns said, "It is a specific person, place, or thing."

Andrew retorted, "Pacific."

"No!" Victoria exclaimed. "Specific!"

"You mean, Pacific?" Andrew again questioned Victoria.

"Exactly," proclaimed Victoria. "Pacific noun." I decided that some things are better left alone!

Even though I tried to avoid idioms in my conversations with the children, they would eventually come out.

"Leopards can't change their spots," "a dime a dozen," "a chip on your shoulder," and "a penny for your thoughts" were statements that brought a lot of laughter into our household. As I was preparing dinner one night, I opened a cabinet, and all the Tupperware fell out. "Someone set a booby-trap," I retorted. The boys looked at me in shock, and they rolled on the floor, roaring with laughter. That was the last time I used that idiom!

School not only brought difficulty in academics but also interesting conversations with their peers. One clear day after school Victoria came home from school and blurted out, "I am on a diet!" With the same breath, she inquisitively said, "What is a diet?"

At times the children would reflect back on their life in Zambia. One evening, for example, Victoria, Andrew, and Andre were intensely arguing over which insects were best to eat. Caterpillars, centipedes, or white termites were their top choices. The debate continued about which bug was the tastiest, and they finally decided that the white bugs were the most delicious.

After much discussion, Andre leaned over, shook his head, and then whispered in my ear, "Caterpillars smell when they are cooked, and they taste really bad." I hoped I was providing the children with a tastier diet at home!

We tried to broaden the children's experiences by taking them to different places, hoping to expand their horizons. One clear spring day we were at the zoo, and prairie dogs popped their heads out of a burrow. Kerry and the boys curiously watched the prairie dogs.

Andrew emphatically stated, "When you see a prairie dog, you wait until it sticks his head out of the burrow and then hit him over the head with a big stick. Then you can eat them." During our tour through the zoo, we visited an African exhibit and passed a grass hut. Andrew inquisitively asked me, "Who lives there?" Kerry shook his head, realizing how far the boys have come from their life in the village.

During the first month the boys lived in America, we ran from appointment to appointment, trying to catch them up on their shots. Victoria, Andrew, and Andre were experiencing their first trips to a dentist and doctor. Since the twins did not have any medical records, they would each receive five shots at a time.

Kerry would tell the boys, "Welcome to America," as the nurses pricked the boys' arms. In addition, the dentist was surprised at the condition of their teeth. Even though the boys had never had a toothbrush, they had straight white teeth. We discovered the reason for their pearly whites was the absence of sugar in their diet, a lack of preservatives, and the tough food that stimulated a strong root system. Andrew and Andre explained to me that they would take bark from a tree and rub their teeth with it to help clean their teeth.

Communication was a challenge for the entire family. We were far from having normal conversations. One winter day Kerry was driving the boys to the doctor for additional shots when Andrew said, "We have a lot of ships in Zambia." Since Zambia is a landlocked country, Kerry chirped back that Zambia may have boats but not ships. Andrew and Kerry continued back and forth about the ships until Andrew looked out the window and said, "There it is with four legs." Andrew was pointing to the sheep, not ships, in the field. Kerry laughed, knowing that this was simply a continuation of our International Twilight Zone.

One January day, I told the boys that we would run to the store. As we headed out the door, Andrew began to sprint down the street. I called him back and asked why he had not gotten into the car. Out of breath, Andrew confusedly said, "Mom, you said we were going to run to the store." After we drove into the parking lot, Andre and Andrew remained in their seatbelts, unwilling to move. Sensing their vulnerability and hesitancy with an unfamiliar environment, I again verbalized each step that would help them to exit the car. "Unbuckle your seatbelt, hold the door handle, open the door, and get out" were step-by-step instructions the boys needed to get out of the car. Then, as they exited, each boy would nonchalantly walk in a different direction, not having a clue where they were going. I would have to grab them by the collar before they wandered into the parking lot like stray puppies. They would walk around the grocery store with a glazed look on their faces, unable to take in all the different items and smells of each aisle, no doubt experiencing sensory overload. A shopping cart became a thrill ride for the boys as they sat in it, hung on it, pretended it was a race car, and then proceeded to ram it into the back of my heels. Needless to say, we tried to avoid shopping together as much as possible in those early days.

Having never experienced cold weather in Zambia, the children had many questions about the Midwest winter like, "Why is it cold outside, but warm inside?", Why does my blanket have duck feathers in it?", and "Why can't I feel my fingers when they are cold?"

In mid-January, when Victoria stepped off the bus after her first day of school, her feet landed on a patch of ice that sent her backpack flying into the air. She scrambled to regain her footing, only to land on her back. Bursting through the door, Victoria announced, "Wow, ice is cold in America."

Another way Midwest winters were difficult for the children: they had to learn how to put on gloves, hats, heavy coats, and boots. They were cold at the slightest drop in temperatures and remained cold all winter, unable to adjust to the change.

Holidays brought a buzz of excitement and new life into our home. "Wow! That is a huge chicken," Andrew exclaimed on Thanksgiving. He had never seen a cooked turkey, and when we had dinner, he enjoyed every bite. Their faces lit up when our family gathered around the fireplace or when we sang around the piano.

For Halloween, Andrew could not figure out why kids wear costumes, thinking dressing up was silly. In addition, the children had never experienced a birthday celebration or gifts for Christmas; therefore, the smallest gift brought exhilaration. Most of all, Andrew and Andre treasured their new family and the security and warmth of a home.

It was refreshing how Andrew and Andre lived for each moment, enjoying the smallest details in life. The boys would entertain themselves for hours on end; they took delight in playing with the smallest objects, such as a piece of chalk or a small pile of rocks. They were thrilled to simply take a walk down the street and lie in the grass to watch the sunset. In contrast to many American families, Zambian children do not expect parents to entertain them or take them places. If we were running errands and they were thirsty, the children would never complain or ever think to ask me to buy them a drink. Even when one of the boys was sick, he would simply lie in bed and never complain. They would not make their needs known, and I would have to prod them to tell me how they felt. In Zambia, if Andrew or Andre were sick, they would silently suffer alone because there was not any medicine to alleviate their pain or anyone to comfort them.

Victoria began to blossom and tried desperately to fit in with the teenage girls in her school. When she was at home, it became obvious that she had missed a few pieces of her childhood in Zambia. She wanted to play with Barbies, watch princess movies, and learn to dance in order to fulfill her childhood dreams. Victoria desperately wanted to recapture the childhood that she lost when facing insurmountable odds. Even though she had learned conversational English, Victoria had not yet mastered academic English. She needed to work hour upon hour on her homework to achieve adequate grades.

The teachers at her school were kind to Victoria and appreciated her sweet demeanor and determination.

Each day I tried to explain to Andrew and Andre what made up a family and how to live with each other. As we

> Polygamy is legal in Zambia, and often if a married man has several wives it is a sign of wealth.

drove past our church, I casually mentioned that their dad was marrying someone today. Without hesitation Andre asked, "How many girlfriends does Dad have?" Without a beat, I told Andre that his dad could only handle one wife, and that was me! I again realized that we had a long road ahead of us.

Almost every conversation we had with the children had its own twists and turns. My other adopted daughter, Brittany, would roll her eyes and shake her head at the comical interchange within our family. At the dinner table one evening Andrew said flatly, "We have goats in Zambia."

Victoria retorted back, "Do you mean coats?"

"No, he said goats," Kerry chimed in.

Andrew said emphatically, "I mean ghosts."

Victoria decided to end the nonsense and said, "Yes, we have ghosts in America, too."

One late morning, snow gently laced the porch as the sun's rays sparkled through the frost in the window. Sleepy-eyed and drowsy, Andre came downstairs and stood quietly before me.

"I had a dream, Mom," Andre stated insistently as our eyes locked.

"What did you dream, Andre?" Surprised by his reference to a dream, I inquired further.

"I dreamed that kids stood around me in a circle, and there was one big person. The big person said to me, 'You have come here for a purpose,'" Andre clearly stated.

My curiosity was aroused, and I asked, "What did you do?"

"I covered my eyes because the light was so bright," Andre said, and he reenacted his dream by covering his face. Then he asked, "What does 'purpose' mean, Mom?"

I stepped back and began to process Andre's dream. The dream helped me realize that Andrew and Andre were not randomly chosen to be part of the Frantz family; God had handpicked them for His purpose.

One late fall day, Kerry and I brought the boys to a neighboring park. A friend who had adopted four children was walking her dog nearby. As we began to chat, she mentioned that for the 2011 tax-year we would qualify for a tax rebate for each child adopted. I was all ears and wanted to know more, "Do you mean a tax deduction?"

"No," my friend said emphatically, "an actual rebate."

Absorbing three new children in our home, coupled with the cost of going to Africa three times, had caused us to go into financial overdrive. Excitedly, week after week, I began to gather all the receipts and paperwork that related to our trips to Africa. All the receipts were recovered except for those from our first trip. Gathering the troops, I assigned each child a section of the house to find the lost receipts. After a long day of unsuccessful searching, Andre paused and put his head down. Andrew faintly whispered, "Mom, if we do not find the papers, will I have to go back to Zambia?"

I stopped my frantic search and hugged Andrew. "Andrew, you will always be our son."

Some things were more important than receipts. I then packaged up all the receipts I could find and sent them to the US government. They were denied, and an enclosed letter stated that we had one last chance to gather and organize more receipts.

A month later and after many sleepless nights, I sent a box of receipts to the US government. The following month our family was gathered in the living room as I opened a letter from the IRS.

After I read the official letter aloud, I said to Kerry, "I do not understand what this means."

As I stood up, a paper dropped out of the envelope and onto the floor. I picked up the piece of paper and tried to make out the amount of the check. I gasped as I read the amount. I looked at Kerry in disbelief and flashed the check in front of him. With excitement, Kerry hugged me and swirled me around. Amazingly, it was a check that covered half the adoption cost! All the children joined in the celebration as we rejoiced in the Lord's goodness to our family.

Meanwhile, Kerry was still determined to tap into any hidden athletic talent the boys had, so he immediately signed up to coach their baseball team. I shook my head at the prospect of the boys being able to field balls, especially since they had never worn a ball glove or swung a bat. Practice was like watching the three stooges as they ran the bases the wrong direction, threw the ball to the wrong base, and stayed in the outfield when the inning was over. Since they did not understand the ball and strike count, they swung at pitches with reckless abandon. At the end of the championship game, Andre was up to bat at the last inning with bases loaded and two outs. I covered my eyes as I heard the umpire yell, "Strike one! Strike two!" Suddenly, I heard a loud crack and realized that Andre had hit the ball out of the ballfield! Kerry jumped up and let out a bellowing shout. Coach Kerry reveled that he had trained star athletes.

Christmas Eve, one month after the boys came to America, we attended our church service. The service was packed, with every seat filled. Christmas decorations glistened in the lights. Following the singing from the exuberant choir, children were called up to the platform to listen to the children's sermon. While they sat quietly on the stairs, the pastor asked them what they wanted for Christmas. Small hands raised, and the children shared their wishes for what type of toys they wanted for Christmas. "I would like a video game," a child answered, excited. Another child eagerly shouted, "I want a new bike!" Sitting quietly in the backrow Andrew and Andre were perched on the top stair. Andre slowly raised his hand. Kerry and I held our breath, not knowing if Andre even understood the question and wondering if he would be able to answer it.

The pastor glanced in the direction of Andre. "Oh no," I whispered to Kerry. We braced ourselves as Andre answered the pastor.

With eyes glistening and a sweet smile on his face, Andre quietly said, "I love my family."

A hush settled over the crowd. A tear rolled down my face, and I glanced up at the cross. The journey was worth it all.

Epilogue

Pastor Bernard and Medica have moved away from the village to Lusaka. Pastor Bernard is currently a Bible teacher. He is in close contact with the orphans of Baluba Village and continues to advocate for the needs of the orphans.

Billiant, who was instrumental in the adoptions, was tragically killed in a bus accident in February 2013 that killed fifty-three passengers. His widow and five children were forced to leave their small home and return to live in the village.

Teri Wilson concluded her ministry for disadvantaged and abused women in Zambia and is currently living in the US.

Victoria's grandfather died in 2014 from high blood pressure. Her grandmother, a widow, was forced to move out of her hut and sadly lost the land she grew vegetables on. She cared for Victoria's two young cousins, whose mother was ill. She also recently went home to Jesus, so she is no longer suffering.

Victoria has suffered from a chronic illness for two years. Victoria's faith has sustained her. In spite of her trials, Victoria has excelled in academics and is a freshman in college studying to be a nurse.

She is determined to "never leave home and take care of us when we are old."

Andre is in eighth grade and is busy with sports and telling his fellow classmates about Jesus.

Andrew is also in eighth grade and hopes to one day to be in full time ministry.

Since their Zambian adoptions, Kerry and Nancy became foster parents to three more boys—Sincere is nine years old, Donte is ten years old, and Elijah is eleven years old. They are in the process of adopting all three boys. Nancy and Kerry now have five athletic boys and two beautiful daughters remaining in the house. Their oldest daughter Cassie is married and has three children. Their oldest son Nate is also married and has a daughter and son. Their daughter Bethany teaches in an elementary Christian school, Brittany works as a chef, and Nancy is still racing to keep up!

Bibliography

Chapter 3

Literacy in a Box Trust, A New Dawn, A New Day: The Rotary Club of Roborough, Plymouth, January 2017, http://www.literacyboxtrust.org.uk/

Chapter 5

Frechette, Richard. *Haiti: The God of Tough Places, the Lord of Burnt Men.* Transaction Publishers, 2012. Print.

Chapter 9

Luciano, Phil. "Dunlap Family Introduces Children to a Whole New World". *Peoria JournalStar,* January 15, 2012: Pages 2. Print.

About the Author

NANCY FRANTZ is a special education teacher, pastor's wife, and mother of ten children. In her book she writes of the emotional ups and downs of parenting, and of her long road to multiple adoptions. She transparently shares a journey that traverses from the lows of jarring disappointment to the joys and challenges of completing her family.

Made in the USA
Columbia, SC
22 September 2017